Ireland's Mr Show Jumping

About the Author

Anne Holland has written more than 20 books, mostly on the subject of horses and in particular horse racing. A successful amateur rider, she won many point-to-points and was one of the first women to ride, and win, under National Hunt Rules in the UK. Anne now lives in rural County Westmeath.

Ireland's Mr Show Jumping

The Life and Times of Frank McGarry

Anne Holland

The Liffey Press

Published by
The Liffey Press Ltd
Raheny Shopping Centre, Second Floor
Raheny, Dublin 5, Ireland
www.theliffeypress.com

A catalogue record of this book is
available from the British Library.

ISBN 978-1-908308-65-8

Printed in Spain by GraphyCems

Contents

Foreword

I have known Frank McGarry since our cattle dealing and exporting days in the 1950s and 1960s, and through his riding
school. He has done a huge amount for the Irish horse, and although Frank has had his ups and downs he remains an honest
to God West of Ireland man, interested in all kinds of activities
and a friend to everybody.

I remember the days when we called him 'Spiv' McGarry
because he was good looking and always well dressed and well
spoken. There was a time when I was standing with a farmer
in Ballycastle Fair, County Mayo, trying to buy cattle from him
when we heard what sounded like an American voice, and then
a well-dressed man rounded the corner. It was Frank McGarry.

I welcome this book about Frank because of the contribution he has made to rural life, and to the horse and show jumping industry. I recommend it as a historical document over a
period of 50 to 60 years. Frank recalls those days with clarity
and his many stories are told with a light and understanding
touch by acclaimed author Anne Holland, and I encourage
readers to buy it.

Ray MacSharry
October 2014

BALLYMAHON SHOW 1967

1

Shipwreck

He held one hand aloft, balancing the wicker basket as best he could in the 20-foot waves while splashing with his other arm and kicking his legs. Another man did the same and between them they kept the basket safe. Inside was a little baby, its mother frantically trying to stay afloat nearby as the sea raged.

It had seemed a normal journey as the island coastline hove into view and a tremor of excitement pulsed through the passengers. For some of them it meant home. For perhaps one or two it beckoned for holiday, visiting family. But its craggy outline brought only dreams of business to one young man. A few days off to enjoy the Inishmaan landscape didn't enter Frank McGarry's head.

They were almost there when the storm brewed suddenly, throwing people around and cattle falling to their knees in their stalls. Their door burst open and some of them escaped on to the deck, causing havoc.

It should have been a short trip, as it usually was. They had already sailed from Galway to Inisheer, the smallest of the isolated Aran Islands off the Galway/Clare coast, and it was only a short hop from there to Inishmaan. The boat, the *Dun Angus,* was loaded with provisions for the islanders. They would never receive them, bar the washed up bounty.

Frank McGarry clung to the rails. He wanted to make his way in the cattle dealing world, and to prove himself right in not taking up the scholarship he could have gone for. This was against his father's advice, who had dreamt of his youngest son becoming a vet.

The youngest of seven sons and four daughters, he was already used to helping his three brothers, known as the McGarry Brothers, cattle exporters, and he was due to deliver a number of cattle that day in early May, 1947, when Frank was in his late teens.

The wind howled some more, the waves built and the boat rocked and swayed as the unforgiving sea got rougher and rougher. The waves were 20 feet high, the boat veered off course and the next moment – BANG – it had hit a rock. Pandemonium ensued. Cattle were thrown into the water. Men and women, 40 to 50 of them all told, clung to whatever they could.

Frank managed to hang on to the listing deck.

'Start saying your prayers,' shouted a passenger, one Jimmy Farrell.

'Everyone was panicking,' Frank recalls.

He watched futile attempts at lowering the lifeboats. There were four of them. The first one fell between the ship and rock and was crushed. The next one nosedived, filled with water and sank. The third took just two men, appointed to go ashore and fetch help, although by that time the shoreline, temptingly close, was filling with anxious viewers. At last the fourth boat was filled with women and set off for shore.

Finally, the captain announced the order to abandon ship, to jump clear of the boat to avoid being sucked under, and to avoid the cattle's thrashing legs. The remaining cattle were freed from the hold. Everyone was panicking. Some clung on to ropes, some tried to swim ashore, to be cut on the rocks, but they all survived.

By now a number of currachs – small fishing boats – were heading towards the stricken passengers. Frank McGarry cannot say how long he was in the water. He was concentrating on helping the baby and staying afloat himself. His lifejacket came loose and caught him under the chin, leaving a cut that should have had 10 to 12 stitches. Then he heard a voice he knew. It was Rory Flaherty, who sometimes helped the young man buy cattle, and on hearing the distressed ship's hooter he had immediately put to sea. Now Frank and the other man handed him the baby and Frank called to the mother.

Far from thanking Frank, she said, 'I see you're going to be saving yourself anyway.' Frank was plucked out of the water by Rory. Once safely on shore, a woman cut a flour bag, soaked it in sea water and put it on Frank's cut chin.

Frank, who was just short of his twentieth birthday, recalls that he was too young to be frightened at the time.

'What frightened me more was when the salvage started,' he remembers. 'People were tapping the drink from the barrels and hiding behind walls. There was no law on the island and they were getting very, very drunk. The bigger island next door, Inishmore, had a king and a priest who were the law. The people, Gaelic speakers, were drinking at the back of ditches, whiskey and Guinness, they were quite boisterous.'

Frank believes he then went mad because he insisted that Rory row Frank across to the larger Inishmore the very same day, in spite of the still high waves. There, the young man was accommodated by a Mrs Colcannon. Hers was a one-room house, but it was warm and dry, and it became Frank's home for the next nine weeks. The first thing he did was hang his wet clothes up on a pitch fork to dry. Rory had provided him with a woollen waistcoat known as a bawneen, woollen pants, and woollen sweater, all made from Aran wool, and pampotees – shoes made from cattle-skin.

There was almost no food because the boat had gone down with the supply of provisions. By a miracle there were no human fatalities.

'There was no bread and no tea; if the hen laid we got an egg. There were no cigarettes. I used to crush oats between two stones and they were put on the stove overnight to make porridge. I fished when it was calm, and we usually had fish and potatoes for lunch, and potatoes and fish for supper.'

On other days Frank walked the 31-square kilometre island. Before long, there was barely a blade of grass he did not know, or a head of cattle he did not recognise. He loved the country life there and reckons he walked round the island several times.

There were a few horses along with the sheep and cattle, and there was one he recognised as a thoroughbred. He was offered it for £18 and with his instinct for dealing he was tempted, but declined. In later years he was told the horse's name was Monaveen – the horse that became the first winner for the Queen Mother and her daughter, Princess Elizabeth (now the Queen) – but the dates do not tally. If he was there at all it would have been a few years earlier (and a pub in Barna was named the Monaveen; it is now called The Twelve Hotel).

Communication with the mainland was nil, although a Sunday paper had published news that the boat had gone down and a picture of it, but gave no mention of survivors. The ferry was wrecked and there was no replacement, no means of getting back, and no phones. It could be a desolate place.

At last, after just over two months, Frank got a lift back to the mainland in a hooker (a turf boat). It landed at Carraroe, and from there he walked the 25 to 30 miles to Galway Harbour where two months before he had parked his prized touring Vauxhall motor car with canvas convertible hood; it started first go after its long lay-off.

Frank used to take his pals in it to the cinema. Now he was driving home, but as he reached the crossroads, when nearly there, a group of boys scattered on seeing him.

'They thought I was a ghost, they all believed I was dead,' he says. 'I opened the back door and my mother, Kate, fainted.'

She was in the kitchen and collapsed into the chair. Her prodigal son had returned, and everyone was happy again.

'It was wonderful after that, especially with the pals. The cattle deal didn't come off, though. They kept the cattle, and the intended deal fell through.'

2

Barefoot

Driving towards Loch Gill and its Isle of Innisfree, made famous in the poem by William Butler Yeats, the driver is unlikely to notice the overgrown remains of a long avenue in a townland called Gorthlownan. In an area of outstanding natural beauty, near Ballintoher in County Sligo and close to the County Leitrim border, this avenue leads to the remains of Frank McGarry's childhood home, though the house where he was born to Jimmy and Kate McGarry has been derelict for half a century. Frank was the youngest of 11 children, nine of whom survived, and grew up near Killery Mountain, a mile from the Isle of Innisfree.

In many ways it was easy growing up. The children simply did as they were bid and anyway they knew what chores were theirs without being told. Frank believes his father had been quite a big farmer at one time but, for whatever reason, he no longer was when Frank was growing up, and then he died when Frank was still quite young. But he had exported cattle to Scotland and at home he grew hay, half an acre of potatoes, enough oats for the house and animals, reared a pig for the pot, milked seven or eight cows, kept two donkeys which acted as tractors, and had a piece of bog on which to bring turf home for the fire.

From as early as six years old Frank knew what he wanted to be – a show jumper. He wanted a pony so much that sometimes he was crying for one.

'You can get that idea out of your head,' his mother frequently told him.

Frank produced an English newspaper cutting with a report of an English team show jumping abroad.

'You're going to see my name jumping for Ireland sometime,' he asserted.

At the time, however, it was only the Irish Army that did any show jumping.

'My dream would have been looked on as a fallacy, the same as flying to the moon because we didn't have a civilian team. The Army were the only people that were invited to go anywhere for the country.'

In time, Frank was to change all that, almost single-handedly, but as a six-year-old boy he was continually pestering his mother for a pony.

'She certainly didn't want me near horses for two reasons. One was that I was going to get killed off one at some stage, and the other was the feeling in the country that people who had horses either had to be paupers or millionaires, and that if you were a millionaire who had a horse you would soon be a pauper.'

Yet Kate (née Gilmartin) loved racing and would have a bet every day of the week in Sligo. Every summer she took the children to Bundoran for three to four weeks. There were bathing boxes on the beach, and they stayed in digs with a relative, Mrs O'Gorman. Included in the £1 and 25 pence cost were three meals a day that nearly always included roast lamb and sometimes fish in the evening, plus crackers and milk at about 10.00

p.m. after a card-playing session. The older children would go dancing in the evenings.

Kate would go to the slot machines in the amusement arcade where she was given a stool and played to her heart's content. When she returned her hands would be black from the coppers. When she was losing her older sons, by then in their twenties, would quietly refurbish her.

In horse-racing she invariably backed whatever Lester Piggott was riding.

'If he was riding a donkey she would still back him,' Frank recalls.

In later years, her sons indulged her hobby; long since widowed, she would worry about a pound. The sons would quietly go to the betting office and pay offer her debts, leaving a small amount of credit in her account.

They would bring her to Mass on a Saturday.

'Don't bring me back,' she would say, 'I have some shopping to do.'

Her sons, reading her, would ask, 'How's the betting?'

Frank recalls, 'She would bet on two flies climbing up a wall.'

Frank remembers his parents as always singing, which is doubtless where he got his good voice from. A choir boy, he once was considered good enough to be an opera singer.

He heard a story about his father from his school teacher later in life concerning an incident in 1922. It was after the civil war and politics were still very strong in every family. Politicians would speak to fair gatherings through the horn of a gramophone player. One time Frank's father, James, known as Jimmy, had had a few drinks and began heckling the speaker, an opposition TD to the Fianna Fáil party to which he belonged. The TD couldn't answer his questions and so he called the guards and asked them to remove McGarry. Jimmy was taken by the collar and escorted down to the barracks.

'What's the charge?' he asked.

'You were interfering with the speech.'

'That's democracy,' Jimmy said.

The young policeman let him go, and Jimmy went back to the pub, drank a bit more and then returned to the fair where the TD was still speaking.

'You are only a shower of bastards,' he called. Once more the police were called, and this time the matter went to court, where Jimmy defended himself.

People came on donkeys and ponies, and in carts, traps and horse-drawn vans from all around to listen. The teacher closed the school so that he could attend, and the courtroom filled in anticipation of what McGarry was going to say.

They were to be disappointed – at first. The clerk read out the case and the judge asked McGarry, 'You have heard the charge, how do you plead?'

'Guilty.'

So he was fined, and walked across the courtroom to pay. As he did so, he turned to the judge and asked, 'May I ask you, can you be fined for thinking?'

'No.'

'Well, I'd like the court and all the people here to know that I still think they're a shower of bastards!'

James McGarry was mainly a farmer and cattle exporter, to Aryshire, but for a spell he worked in a Scottish brickyard for 11 shillings a week for 12 hours a day. After he came home he met and married Kate Gilmartin; she was 18 years old and he was in his early thirties.

They were a light-hearted couple and music played a big part in the house at Gorthlownan, Sligo, where Frank grew up. It was part thatched and part slate-roofed, with no electricity. Homework was done by candlelight. The candles were made by peeling rushes, twisting them and dipping them into beef fat. James McGarry was nearly always under the lamp reading, especially Thomas Hardy novels; he would write letters for the illiterate. All eleven children were delivered at home by a handywoman/midwife, Mrs Frizzell.

'She was a Protestant and a wonderful woman,' Frank recalls. 'She would walk across the fields in clogs, and then change into a dress and high heels when she got here. If my mother was sick she took over; my father was a little afraid of her. It might be 6.00 a.m. and she would tell him to "get out and do some work". Mother kept a chest that contained two candles and two starched sheets which Mrs Frizzell used for babies arriving or corpses going out.'

James McGarry ensured his children had good posture by making them walk round the circular parlour table with a book on their heads, and then jog. He was also very keen on diction and the children had to pronounce everything properly.

He was well respected and, an unqualified vet, he would castrate and de-horn young bulls for local farmers, and cures for ailments were passed down the generations. He liked hunting, and attended the local fairs wearing breeches and leggings, as was the norm. There were driving ponies and donkeys around the place, and unbeknown to Frank as a child his paternal grandfather had spent a lifetime with horses.

Frank used to cycle to buy a daily newspaper for a penny for his father, but when its price increased to three halfpence, he only got one on alternate days with his neighbour Agnes, and the two of them started swapping.

School for Frank was at Crossboy with about 90 pupils divided into three classrooms, and two teachers, Charlie McMorrow, the head, and his wife. Frank remembers him as a very religious man who taught them a lot about the Gospel.

'I learnt a lot of things from him and his wife that I've never forgotten.'

He was five years old when he started school, his mother having held on to him, being the youngest, until one day Mrs McMorrow said to her, 'He'll be shaving if you don't get him to school pretty shortly.'

Although bright, Frank did not much enjoy school. Kate McGarry used to threaten her youngest son with the stick to get him to go to school, with his little Woolworth's bag that had cost sixpence. It contained his lunch, bottle of milk, exercise book and prayer book.

This is where Frank went to school – the roads were sandy tracks

Frank was not used to interaction with other children, and he found they played rough, which again he had not experienced before. Nevertheless, he soon settled in and made many lifelong friends.

One was Ultan and they walked the mile to school together, in the summer time in bare feet. This wasn't because they couldn't afford shoes but because it was de rigueur among the children to walk barefoot from May 1, and they would jeer at anyone who came in shoes. The roads had no tarmac, but were sandy and soft.

'We played football in bare feet, on the road at lunchtime, and we didn't wear shoes again until September,' Frank recalls. The soles of their feet became well-hardenend. The roads began to be chipped and tarred when he was about eight or nine.

Frank's pal Ultan McMorrow, son of the teacher,
his brother Pat Joe and Frank

One day his ankle was injured playing football. He tried to ignore it and carry on, but as a result he got blood poisoning. So he rode the donkey to school, and left it in a paddock by the school garden during the day. He got jeered at because he wasn't walking – but it started him riding other than on the bog.

His father taught him one of life's lessons when Frank was playing football. Frank might say, 'We're only one goal down,' and his father would reply, 'Yeah, I know, but it'll take two goals to catch up, you'll have to score two before you're better.'

Frank's father Jimmy

Frank says, 'He was a wonderful father and very good at rearing kids. He was a very intelligent man with a great attitude, and would let me do my own thing without checking me.'

He kept a well-stocked vegetable garden. 'Everything you've ever heard of in a garden, he had it,' Frank says. 'He was a great herbalist as well.'

One of his father's favourite soups was based on rabbit, or hare in season – a hunting and shooting man, he wouldn't dream of shooting anything off season. The hare soup was something of a ritual which his mother hated, involving hanging and gutting and skinning, but his father loved it. The flesh was nearly like venison, which they also had occasionally. Sometimes a snipe was also put into the hare soup, and always onions, carrots, parsnips, leeks, turnips, white turnips and seasoning.

Watercress was on the menu in the spring, often as a vegetable. Potatoes were abundant. Lamb came in at Easter, winter cabbages in November, and curly kale which wasn't picked until it had had a frost on it. Leeks, celery and spring greens all were eaten in season.

Rabbits were plentiful, being before the myxomatosis disease that nearly wiped them out in the 1950s, and were cooked in many different ways by Kate McGarry, including roasted, or rabbit with bacon, or boiled in soup.

Bread was homemade, too, often with additions like raisins and bran, and Frank believes or was ten or twelve years old before he ever ate any bread from a bakery. He remembers the hundredweight linen sacks of flour being delivered to the house, and the names displayed across them: Millocrat, Early Dawn, and Pride of the West. When the flour was gone, Frank's mother bleached the sacks to get rid of the printed names and turn them white. She then stitched them together to make bed sheets, and sometimes school shirts.

'She was a very good seamstress, and she had to be economic,' says Frank. 'After all, she had eleven children.'

Slimming and ill-health were two things that virtually didn't exist in the country children.

'There was no poverty and no dirt in the country, unlike the poverty and filth in a city. We might have dirty clothes coming in in the evening from the mud of the fields, but it wasn't dirt as such.'

Country boys and girls all had healthy complexions. At 16 years old Frank weighed 11 stone, 11 pounds, and he has remained the same every decade ever since.

'If you kept working you didn't have to slim. You got your vitamins from the food, you exercised and worked it off.'

The killing of the home pig was something of a ritual. It had been fed on Indian meal, apples, boiled potatoes and oats, which resulted in sweet and aromatic meat, and was three or four months old, weighing eight or nine stone. On the appointed day the butcher arrived with an array of knives and scrapers.

'He had a big black waterproof on him and I started to cry because I thought I was going to get killed. We all watched the killing of the pig. It was bound hand and foot and he just cut its throat, hung him up and allowed the blood to go. Of course, the blood was saved as well. Mother was squeamish, and I suppose we were all a bit squeamish – but it was a wonderful day, the day the pig was killed.'

The pig was washed and its hair was shaved off him with the scraper, and then put into hot water, so it looked white when hanging.

A few days later the butcher came again, and the pig was cut down and cut into joints. Hams were boned if requested, and the crewbeans (the feet and shins) were taken off and put aside, either for soup or to give away. All the neighbours were given a number of spare ribs, and sometimes a neighbour would be given half the head, which had also been shaved. Once all the parts had been butchered they were laid down in a barrel of salt. This produced brine and after three to four weeks the various cuts were hung on hooks from the roof, ready for rashers of bacon to be cut off.

'When I was coming in from the fields or from riding my pony you could smell it cooking from a long way off. It was really wonderful bacon; a sweeter meat you couldn't have eaten and nothing like today when a white froth comes out of it and all that water used to make it weigh more.'

Friday was fish day, and it was sometimes also eaten mid-week. It was brought round by fish men in a little pony and cart containing herring, whiting, plaice, brill and so on.

As a child, Frank recalls, 'We knew everything about the flowers and the birds and the bees, and everything was absolutely normal. There was nothing awesome about any part of the birds or the bees, or the cows or bulls, and the stallions and the mares, it was all just normal. We didn't have to learn about things out of books, they were all there in the fields for us.'

With a friend or two he would watch the birds' nests and they would keep their locations secret from anyone else.

From an early age Frank wrote poetry, something he has continued with all his life, and he was about eight when he wrote this one:

The little bird sat on the nest of four
Eggs of blue and darkened spots all o'er
As a child I watched her seek her little prey
And saw her nest twice or more each day.

One by one, the little beaks started to appear
And mother spread her wings whenever I got near;
From a broken shell, a brand new life begun
My world became a better place when that fledgling sung.

Father sat on a branch way up high
And watched the mother teach them how to fly,
He sometimes helped the hen or youths to feed,
Why can't we humans, these little birds give heed.

Wings grew and abandoned nest was seen
A vacant gap within my life, sorrow in between,
The one I'd held upon my hand, floating in the air
Another song, another life, another love, elsewhere.

At about the same age Frank used to do a children's puzzle in the English newspaper that his father had, but he could seldom send it in because it had an entry fee of sixpence, which he didn't have. One time the competition was to put three lines of verse in front of the line, 'he ain't built that way'. The first prize was £1, an enormous sum to the young boy. He composed the lines and asked his father for the fee, but he would only hand it over if Frank read him his three lines. Reluctantly, he did so.

A man can laugh through the whole of a farce
A man can laugh through the whole of a play
But a man cannot laugh through the hole of his arse
He ain't built that way.

Jimmy McGarry laughed out loud, gave the sixpence – and Frank won the prize.

3

Living the Seasons

Writing poetry and songs for stage and concerts was to become an integral part of Frank's life, as we shall see, but as a child it was mainly a life out of doors, helping on the farm, playing football or organising secret impromptu donkey races – secret because he couldn't let his mother know of some of the falls he took.

After school and homework, the jobs depended on the season, and this was often a case of all the neighbours helping each other. For instance, once one person's hay was cut, they would go on to the next, all hands – and donkeys and rudimentary machinery – on deck.

When it was turf cutting time, around Easter, Frank's job, along with other children, was to scatter the turf 'bricks' for drying by the roadside; they were brought there by teams of donkeys. The following day they stood them up in groups of five, known as 'footing', unless the weather was wet, in which case they clamped them like a hay stook. They were left there until the autumn (thieving was almost unknown) when again all the neighbours chipped in with their donkeys to draw them home. Like all little boys then, Frank wore short trousers, but that didn't stop him riding the donkeys either side-saddle or astride. If he rode side-saddle Frank discovered that he could prevent his bare knees from being rubbed by the creels, the corners of the baskets straddled each side of the donkey. Before long Frank discovered he could stand up on a galloping donkey without losing balance.

While working on the bog Jimmy McGarry would make a fire and boil a can of water to make tea, adding a handful of leaves to make it strong. A loaf of bread was spread with rhubarb jam, and eggs were boiled in the can.

There was a three-day spell working on the bog for one of the neighbours, Tommy John McGarry (no relation), when Frank was about 14, filling in for an older brother who was ill. This neighbour picked Frank up at 5.00 a.m. and by the time they reached the bog about three miles away he was feeling hungry – but there was no time for food. It was straight into catching the turf sods as the neighbour cut and threw them out of the ditch, placing them in the barrow and wheeling it away when full. If he failed to catch a sod it might hit him in the face. Before long, sweat was rolling off him and he was covered in black.

At last 12 noon came and time for lunch, which was a mug of tea, bread and jam then it was on with the hard labour. Frank heard a train in the distance. He knew there was one at 5.00 p.m. and another at 8.30 p.m. He hoped it was the later train, but no luck, and the work continued. At last it was time to go home on the cart – sitting on top of the pile of turfs was luxury to his stiff and aching limbs – and then it was straight into the galvanised tin bath. It all started again at five the next morning, and lasted for three days.

The hay was generally cut by a contractor. Frank's job, along with children from neighbouring families, was to follow the mowing machine with a rake and spread it out; this was followed by turning it with forks. When it was ready, hay ricks were built. Frank's favourite job was when he was allowed to take the reins of the horse pulling the hay cart, a great sensation for him. He would pull up a cock of hay, and it was forked up to a man on the cart. At the end of the day there might be sixty or seventy cocks to go into the rig of hay.

'It would be trimmed and my father would pluck that rig down at the bottom. He'd have a foundation of stone, covered in cut bushes, to prevent the hay getting rotten on the ground. It was a big art, because it had to be shaped so the rain ran down off it and didn't get down to the underneath part, so it had to run off the part that was thatched like a house.

'It was thatched with cut rush which my father had. Others had oaten straw or barley straw, and then it was roped. It was maybe twenty feet high and the ropes had to go around. It was artistically done, without so much as half an inch variance in the ropes going round and round; the ropes were a red twine. This was followed by roping from the bottom right over to the other side and tied, about nine inches apart. Thus it was tied down for the winter.'

Once all this was done, all around the neighbourhood, the completion was celebrated with half a barrel of Guinness, and maybe brandy and whiskey, and plenty of food. There might also be an impromptu *céilí*. The dancing and drinking and joke telling would go on long into the evening in the kitchen. At about 2.00 a.m. a number of the fellows would have to tack up their horses again and drive home.

Potato picking in October, around Halloween time, was a back-breaking job, but there was no escaping it.

'If it started to rain you had to dig them anyway. There were no tractors to do it. They were dug out and we had to pick them when we came home from school.'

There might be 20 ridges of potatoes dug anywhere between 200 to 400 yards long. The boys had to pick up the big ones for the house, and leave smaller or bad ones. Once the big ones had been bagged and taken away the boys then had to pick the small ones for the hens and pigs. One job Frank never had to do (or managed to get out of it) was the twice-daily milking of the cows.

At about ten or eleven he also found the fun – and the profit – in rabbitting. A chum of his, Michael James Clancy, known as Sneezer, from Tubber an Aine, about a mile from Frank's house, had a sheepdog, and one day he suggested to Frank that they could sell rabbits, if they could catch them.

Frank says, 'In those days you didn't see money. If you were lucky you might get two pence at Easter and maybe sixpence at Christmas, this at the time when there were 240 pence to one pound!'

The two lads set off on a Saturday morning with the dog and two spades to where the rabbit burrows were. When the dog pawed at a hole the boys knew a rabbit was at home and set about digging it out, knocking it on the head, and adding it to their growing collection.

Where roots made it too hard for them to dig they cut a piece of briar, pushed it down the hole, twisted it and pulled it back, usually with a wriggling rabbit on the other end, its fur caught up in the briar. They took them home, gutted them, and agreed to try selling them to a man with a horse and cart called McDaniel from Sligo, father of a successful singer called Maisie who had several records to her name.

Michael James took them to him on Saturday night, and so it wasn't until school on Monday morning, before lessons started, that Frank caught up with him again, and asked how he had got on.

'Here's your share,' said Michael James, and he handed Frank a red ten shilling note. It was an enormous amount of money and Frank was so thrilled with it that he put it in a box at home. Sometimes he took it out to admire it.

'That was the most precious thing I had in my lifetime until then,' Frank recalls, 'and it took a lot to get me to cash that one – that was a prisoner.'

Meanwhile, the rabbitting continued regularly on Saturdays, and it brought not only decent pocket money, almost a living, but it taught Frank the rudiments of bargaining, too. They learnt to barter with McDaniel, who might offer sixpence; they would try for a shilling and end up accepting ninepence. But rabbits whose fur had been mauled by the dog, they learnt, were worth nearly nothing, so they took more care about that.

The boys' friends, seeing how many ten shilling notes they were getting, decided to get in on the act, too, sometimes ten, twelve or even fifteen of them. It was time for more good advice from Jimmy McGarry to his youngest son.

'Where are you going today?'

'To Baun, after rabbits.'

'Are you all going after rabbits?'

'We are.'

'Well, take my advice now,' Jimmy McGarry said. 'If there's ten or twelve of you going up that road after rabbits, you turn and go down the other road. There mightn't be as many rabbits, but you'll only have to get one, whereas there'll have to be twelve or thirteen up there for you to get one each, and if you get two, you'll be better off.'

Frank was about twelve when he bought his first calf. He was at a fair in Drumahair with his uncle, James Gilmartin, and he had £2/10 shillings in his pocket from selling two lambs. He wandered around the fair, and bought a six-month old calf for £1/10-. Later he saw his father and showed him the calf.

'Well, you're a great little boy, now go off and see if you can buy a comrade the very same, and when you have bought two and sold two, you'll be a wiser man.'

At the time, Frank didn't realise he had bought two paltry specimens. He fed and looked after them for six months, giving them porridge, meal, grass and hay. But when he came to sell them six months later he couldn't find any buyers.

'I found I was a much better customer buying them than I was a seller, and I never forgot my father's advice. He said, "The day you buy is the day you sell. You've discovered the two you bought are not the sort you'll buy next time." I thought that was great. He didn't chide me in any way for what I'd done; he let me do what I wanted to do myself, and he said I'd never learn younger!'

Far from putting him off, young Frank soon became addicted to fairs.

Entrepreneurism, a business brain and the will to win were part of Frank's psyche from an early age, not only the rabbitting and calf dealing, but also in organising childhood donkey races.

A middle brother, Danny, already an adult and living in London when Frank was a child, gave him his first donkey. A regular drove of a hundred or more donkeys came from the west, probably Connemara, brought along by gypsies, dealers and the likes. A big man in a hat called Maloney appeared to be in overall charge, travelling in a cart or a horse-drawn caravan, probably on his way to Manorhamilton, Leitrim, or the border towns, to sell them.

Frank's brother bought one for seven shillings and six-pence, a large sum for a donkey at the time, especially as it was barely more than a foal, and gave him to Frank. This is the animal on which Frank really began riding. He still has the photograph of his Confirmation, and there is the donkey in the background.

'I was very attached to the donkey, and rode her before I got a pony.'

In what seemed no time, Frank was organising donkey racing on the road, in the evenings after school or on a Saturday. They picked a start and finish point on the stony, sandy roads

Frank, aged 12, at his Confirmation – Josephine, Rose, Danny, Frank, Kathleen, Moira McMorrow, Maura McMorrow and Annie Gilmartin – with his donkey Bess in the background and their greyhound Swift

and ran in heats of about six, followed by a final. None of them had saddles or even bridles.

'There was no prize money or anything, it was just the point of winning. Coming first was all that mattered to me. I had to win very badly.'

Whips were not allowed (though many boys used them surreptitiously) but Frank found his own way of making a donkey go faster.

'I used to sit on the back of the donkey because the hind legs are the strongest part, and could carry you better than the front legs, and not the middle where the centre of gravity didn't come into it. We had so many falls, and as we had short pants we often came home with knees and elbows cut, and sometimes the nose as well.'

It was the same when ponies came into his life, and there was one particular fall that Frank took care to hide from his mother ...

4

Pony Mad

The farm pony called Black Beauty was Frank's step up from riding donkeys. His main role in life was pulling the cart on farm jobs, or the trap to church on Sundays, but before long Frank was organising point-to-points with his pals and their ponies, usually on a Sunday afternoon, riding Black Beauty himself. The course would start on the McGarry land and could take them as far as the railway, ten farms away, a distance of two or three miles, and back again.

'We just jumped a fence as we came to it, no one checked for barbed wire or anything.'

After the racing, the lads would hold jumping competitions over the walls and hedges, and the more they fell off the more laughs they had, especially if a boy fell into a hedge of briars. Sometimes they attempted to jump obstacles that were impossible for little ponies.

There was one fall that Frank kept from his mother. He and his cousin Dan Gilmartin were racing each other towards a narrow gap. Frank was just ahead but his pony came down in the mud and Dan's pony following close behind in full gallop trod on the fallen Frank.

It left a large mark the shape of a horseshoe on his chest and was in fact so serious that it oozed blood and pus for a long time, sometimes seeping through his shirt. It was sore, too, but Frank made sure he had his bath or shower without being seen.

'I could never show it to my mother or I would have been banned from riding.'

Another fall was very much in public view. He was a young fella and the family had some relations over from Glasgow. Over dinner Jimmy McGarry told them that his youngest son had started riding a pony.

The boreen leading to Frank's childhood home – he overturned the pony and cart turning into it too fast

Frank takes up the story. 'I took the pony out to show off to my Scot friends. There was a nice stone wall between two fields where the hay was, and I cantered down towards the wall, but the pony stopped and I went straight onto my head on the hard ground, and I was humiliated.'

Frank was about twelve when he was first allowed to count the cattle in the evening on horseback. By this time, with his older brothers also farming, they had around 200 acres rented in the area.

He would tack up Black Beauty and set off around the acres. He loved it. The sights and sounds of the countryside, and the smell of his pony and the leather tack. One chore he never demurred from was cleaning the harness ready for Sunday. Every part was dismantled, and oiled and saddle-soaped individually;

the buckles and harness brasses were polished with Brasso. After the polish or dubbin was applied the leather was polished to a shine with a cloth, and then it was on to cleaning the trap, ready for taking the family to church on Sunday.

Church was a part of his young life, including being a choir boy; in later years in Glasgow he met Josef Locke, son of a Northern Ireland cattle dealer, and he recorded a vinyl record of Handel's 'Where 'ere Ye Walk', with 'My Lagan Love' on the B side. Josef's real name was Joseph McLoughlan, and Frank also got to know two of his brothers, Paddy and Tom, the trio singing as the McLoughlan Brothers.

They met in a Sligo Hotel and again the next morning at the fair in Dromore West. The McLoughlans asked Frank to estimate what several bunches of cattle would make. Frank was spot on with his predictions, and so they asked him to buy cattle for them, an order which became regular right up until he retired from the business.

Frank gave serious, if fleeting, thought to becoming an opera singer. But horses and cattle were always his first love.

Frank's love of speed was more than once almost the undoing of Black Beauty when pulling the trap. One time he was returning with a load of baking flour, Indian meal, oatmeal and flax, all of them in hundredweight bags. He had taken the trap, feeling the cart was not smart enough, and put two of the bags into its well, and two beside him which, given his light weight, made it very imbalanced. Regardless of the load, Frank urged Black Beauty faster and faster on the nearly empty roads until, taking the turn into the avenue for home too sharply at the speed they were going, over they turned, trap, bags, pony and Frank, tumbling into the field below the drive. A wheel and spokes were broken, and the only way he got away with it was because he had been on an errand. He was cautioned severely by his father, of course, and the trap itself was away a long time for rebuilding. Brownes of Sligo were tasked with rebuilding the wheel with a specific hardwood.

It wasn't the only time they overturned. Among a number of near-misses was the time he was carrying potato seedlings ready for planting, with Paddy Gallagher, who worked for them and would come over when Frank was out of school. He was driving the cart full of potato seedlings out to the field where they were to be planted, with Paddy beside him. He should only have been walking with such a load but that wasn't fast enough for him. On, on he urged Black Beauty. He had got to the bottom of a ploughed field when he was confronted by a 'green patch' (headland, where the plough had turned) and over they turned, Paddy and Frank beneath the cart and the pony plunging forward. Eventually they got out relatively unscathed themselves, but the cart was damaged and Black Beauty was slightly hurt, too.

After Black Beauty, Frank ventured into his first horse deal. He was about 12 years old. He had heard of a pony for sale and set off on his sports bicycle to see it, liked it and wanted to buy it. The trouble was the price of £4, more than Frank had in the world. He had bought his bike for £1/10-, but told the vendor it had cost £2/10 and, with an extra pound, the pony was his. The man gave Frank a piece of rope and Frank set off to ride him, bareback and without a bridle, the nine or ten miles home. The pony was rather thin so his spine dug into Frank's bum and left him pretty sore – not that that stopped him from trotting flat out all the way home.

To help put weight on him Frank fed him two pounds of oats every morning before going off to school. Once he was in better condition Jimmy McGarry suggested that his son take him to Ballisodare Horse Fair, which he did, and netted £9 for him, a handsome profit. Frank felt a real man, and promptly went on round the fair looking for another one. He found and bought another black one but when he showed it to his father he said, 'Now, son, you're going to have a longer spell to get that one sold, because it's not right.' Jimmy McGarry took the pony back to the seller, who accepted it.

Before long Frank heard of another one and, without telling his family, he took the farm pony, Black Beauty, and cart to go and see it. It was snow white and the fastest trotter he had ever seen. He was mad for it and to buy it he parted not only with his own money but also the family pony, which wasn't his to give, and set sail for home at the speed of light.

He stabled the pony and went to bed, but didn't sleep much wondering what sort of reaction he was going to get. At first, all was well. He told his father and oldest brother, Pat Joe, what he'd done. Jimmy looked at his acquisition and said he seemed sound, though he was unsure about his wind.

'It seems good enough,' he said.

'Wait till you see it in the trap,' Frank said, 'it's a fantastic trotter.'

'It has good movement all right,' Jimmy agreed.

It was a Sunday morning and in no time, with Frank holding the reins and Pat Joe in the trap, he was showing off, passing all the other families on their way to Mass.

'Try and stay behind, it's going to run away.' Pat Joe was somewhat alarmed, but Frank just urged the pony faster, shouting and getting past the other traps.

They reached the village and Pat Joe told his youngest brother, 'Put him in a stable and for God's sake, we can't go home until everybody has gone off the roads because you'll kill children and everything with this pony because you won't be able to stop.'

After Mass they drove to some cattle in the other direction which Pat Joe inspected while Frank held on to the now restless pony.

Trouble set in on the return journey. The pony was a bit bigger than the last one and the trap was a little small for it. With the pony's extravagant action her hind heels were hitting the well of the trap until eventually she smashed right through it. One leg got hung up right beside her human passengers. She panicked, smashing the trap to smithereens until she wriggled out of the harness and galloped home, leaving Pat Joe and Frank to manhandle the wrecked trap back up the long, steep avenue to home.

'Take the pony back to the man,' Jimmy McGarry ordered Frank, 'and get your money and our pony back, and don't do any deals like that ever again.'

So it was back to the seller, this time in the farm cart, where Frank was told by the man, 'You did a deal. I'll give you back your pony but you'll not get back any money.'

It was a chastening lesson for Frank, in which he had now lost all the profit he had made on his first pony deal.

Frank remembers when the nearby village of Dromahair became the first place locally to have electricity, courtesy of the German owner of the Abbey Hotel. He put a turbine in the river and lit the whole village. The new street lamp post became a gathering point for the local youths.

Sometimes they would find a copy of the *Flirting News* tucked behind a stone from which they would learn in verse all the latest gossip about who was dating whom, little guessing it was one of their own number, Frank, who was writing it.

As time went on, Frank always wrote a song for the annual concert, and it invariably brought in a number of local characters and was eagerly anticipated each year.

Frank was about 15 or 16 years old when he bought his first show jumping pony in partnership with an older friend called Freddy McGettrick. The pony cost £22, a big investment, and they called it Rock Prince, because Freddy came from near the Rock of Ballymoate. He was ridden in competitions by Frank's cousin Seamus Gilmartin, with Frank setting a pattern that was continue through his life by schooling him at home. The pony never knocked down a fence but he had one problem: he would always run out at the stone wall.

Frank came up with a bizarre idea: they would try jumping it over a wall at night, Frank's theory being that he wouldn't see the obstacle until it was too late to run out. They both thought that whoever rode it might get killed. They discussed how one would get the other, presumably injured, one out, and they tossed a penny to see who would ride. The result was Frank, and he was up for it. He galloped the pony so hard that by the time he got to the wall he was going too fast to stop, and jumped it.

He landed in a field of flags (wild irises) and the noise of them flapping against the pony's legs made him run off. Once Frank got the pony turned round he jumped the wall back again.

'I jumped the wall both ways several times in the darkness.'

Frank was offered about £17 for him for meat, which he refused to do, but he decided he would sell the pony (but not for meat) if he still refused to jump the wall in a competition. They took Rock Prince to a gymkhana at nearby Dromahair. The night time ruse worked. Rock Prince went in for three competitions without turning a hair at the wall, and won all three with clear rounds. Frank still has the cup.

As he continued on his winning ways potential buyers became interested in him, but Frank was not for selling. A couple stayed at nearby Markree Castle, Collooney, and visited him, saying they were prepared to pay a good price.

'It doesn't matter, I'm putting no price on the pony, I'm not selling him.'

Rock Prince was probably now worth about £70 to £100. The couple persisted and thinking to finally put them off, Frank said, 'unless I get £500 for him, I wouldn't sell,' and the people left.

It was only the next day that Frank discovered the couple were the Duke and Duchess of Norfolk, from Arundel Castle in Sussex, but when they came back he was still adamant that it was £500 or nothing and again they left.

A few days later the steward from Markree Castle met Frank, and asked if he had sold the pony. When Frank replied no, the steward said, 'Well, don't quote me, but I think the boss has got a cheque for you.'

A stunned Frank realised he was going to get the full price, and the Duke confirmed it later. He was buying it for his daughter Lady Sarah Fitzalan-Howard.

'It was my first introduction into big money, for my first jumping pony.'

5

*The Toss of a Coin
– College or Cattle?*

Sixteen-year-old Frank hid behind a hedge, not for the first time, listening to his father and Charlie McMorrow, his head teacher, talking. Yet again the head was telling Jimmy McGarry that his youngest son had enough brains to go to college, and urging him to send him. Either Terenure or Blackrock was discussed, and McMorrow suggested that with Frank's love of cattle and horses a career as a veterinary surgeon, embracing both, might be the best solution. Two scholarships were given from the county, one for a girl and one for a boy, and it was considered Frank could win the latter.

But Frank was already keen to be his own boss. From six years old he had harboured dreams of being a show jumper and in the cattle business, and he never wavered in his ambitions. He told his father he didn't want to go to college.

Jimmy McGarry didn't put pressure on him. He called him in for a talk and said, 'I don't have any money to give you a start in life. With a scholarship we could get you through college but if you want to do the other that's fine, go ahead with your own money, but don't come back here expecting sympathy if it doesn't work out.'

All the money Frank had at the time was £3 or £4, but he knew what he wanted to do and he was determined to succeed.

'I never thought I was going to be a failure, but neither did I expect to make big money or millions.'

Not even his previous experience involving a complex trip to England would put him off the cattle trade. That was when a brother, Danny, in England was ill and couldn't get to a number of cattle markets which were essential for his export business. Another brother, John, decided to send Frank over.

'Of course, being a generation older than I was, I felt obliged to do whatever he said.'

The next three days were spent racing around trying to obtain a passport, and as he wasn't old enough for one a couple of years was added to his age on the application. It was signed by the sergeant in Collooney Barracks who accompanied John into Sligo to get the certificate and send it to Dublin. Ever since then, Frank has celebrated his birthday on May 22 in accordance with his altered birth certificate, instead of his real date of May 18.

The journey over was far from straight forward, especially for a young fella travelling for the first time. Frank took the train from Sligo, through Leitrim up to Enniskillen where he had to change for Omagh, and then again for Belfast. There, he had to change to another station to get the train to the ferry port at Larne. It was shortly before the end of WWII when mines were still in the sea and black out was still in operation, so there were no lights, and Frank fell asleep. When he woke up he asked a porter how much longer it was until they reached Larne.

'Larne? This train is going to Belfast.'

The train had already been to Larne while Frank slept and was now heading back to Belfast. The porter got the train stopped at the next station from where Frank took a taxi back to the port. He was under strict instructions from his family to travel saloon and not steerage, but when he got there the saloon gangway had already been taken up, so steerage it was. There were still mines in the sea, and Frank didn't sleep a wink.

Once in Stranraer, it was another train down to Carlisle, and by the time he got there it was about 10.00 p.m. The cost for the return journey fares over and back totalled £3.

He set off to walk to his brother's address, 222 Homehead Road, but there were no signs and no street lights because of the black out. Eventually, a policeman directed him and after about an hour he found 221 Homehead Road and 223 Homehead Road, and 225, but of 222 there was no sign. Frank walked up and down that road all night until five or six in the morning when daylight came and Frank again asked a policeman. That was when he discovered that even numbers were on the other side of the road.

The landlady got up to let him in and his brother, far from being consoling, tore a strip off him.

'He gave me a dressing down for being late and keeping them up all night, but there was no word about my being up all night.'

Instead, Frank was told to wash, change and get straight on the bus down to the first market at Morpeth. Catching the bus was fraught, too, because Frank was looking for the name of the market without realising that a big town name appeared on the front of the bus, not the small market town which was a stop on the way, so he missed two or three before he got on his way.

Frank was to sell 100 cattle at several northern markets and all he knew was the average price of them. The McGarry-bought cattle arrived at the markets in a number of wagons from far and wide, all of them from fairs in Ireland, assembled at Collooney. These ones had not only had sea and train voyages, but they were also quarantined for 24 hours in Glasgow with little to eat.

'So I had to weigh up each particular wagon on its own and try and sell them to the best of my ability.'

He had to draw (select) the best 12 to 15 animals according to size and quality to make up one lot, and then the next best, and so on through the hundred until they were all penned in their lots. This was only the beginning.

'They were all muck and dirt from the wagons and the shipping, so I had to hose every one of them down, and card out all the muck from their hair.'

That process took hours but his work was not over yet. He was now covered in muck himself, and before they went into the sales ring he would put the finishing touches to them. He might receive a telegram from home saying the cattle stood them in at £80 a head. Transport over had cost £1/10- to £2 per head, so he had to realise £86 for the best lot, £85 for the next and so on, attempting to achieve an average of £83 in order to make an overall profit.

So that was the Wednesday market. Then it was off to Scots Gap in Scotland for the next day, and the whole process all over again. Alnwick in Northumberland was the Friday venue and back to Carlisle on Saturday. Monday and Tuesday it was a two-day sale at Castle Douglas in Scotland and back again to Morpeth on Wednesday. By the time Saturday came Frank had been to eight or nine markets – places such as Perth, Forfar, Montrose, Arbroath, Aberdeen – with the same hard work at each one, and with almost all of the cattle sold. Then it was back on the trains and the ferry for the two-day journey home. Frank had meals on board and he also did up the books of his week and a half's work.

He had gone over little more than a boy, and returned a man. Far from putting him off, he couldn't wait to make this work his life.

Now, having turned down the opportunity of college, Frank was on his own. It didn't start well.

He would buy top quality Aberdeen Angus, a first cross in Sligo at the time, at what he thought was the cheapest market and take them on to another fair the next day to sell at a profit. This way he began building up a clientele who knew the type of animal to expect from him. A pub beside the coast road in Farniharpy was his favourite place for selling. Other than leaving himself a pound for food and lodgings, Frank spent every penny he had on buying more cattle, using money to make money.

He was not afraid of walking long distances. One of the furthest droves of cattle Frank ever undertook on foot was from Maam Cross back home to Sligo, a journey of some 84 miles that took three days and two nights.

Frank bought about 40 little Connemara black cattle. Maam Cross had one house which was also a shop, Peacockes, but by the time Frank had finished buying cattle all the food had gone. He had left home at 5.00 a.m. and was hungry. The two young men then knocked on the door of a slated house to see if they could have some bread and tea. The householder had no bread, but said they could pick some strawberries. Frank was with a fellow dealer called Lang, and they had no option but to head off over the mountains towards Ballinrobe. There were no roadside fences to keep the cattle together, and the pair of them ran nearly as fast as sheepdogs keeping them together and away from the bog holes.

They reached Ballinrobe at about 11.30 p.m. and were told they could house the cattle overnight in Flannerys yard for sixpence a head to include some feed. They found a man called Tommy Kiernan who could put them up, and he boiled them a pot of potatoes to eat and gave them two jugs of milk. The tariff was meant to include breakfast, but that was not available until 10.00 a.m. and by 7.00 a.m. they were back on the road.

Two more days of walking were ahead of them, overnighting at Claremorris. By now they had wrapped the feet of many of the young cattle in jute bags, kept in place with tar to make boots for them on the long trek.

On another occasion, coming from a fair, a heavy fall of snow blocked the road and Frank and a young cattle exporter named Ray MacSharry walked from Strokestown to Boyle, a distance of about 22 miles. From there they were able to catch a train home to Sligo.

Ray remembers a time when someone admired the coat Frank was wearing. 'It had come from a second-hand shop, and it went on his bed at night to keep him warm,' he says.

Ray MacSharry went on to become an eminent politician, with posts that included Tánaiste (deputy Prime Minister), Minister for Agriculture, Minister for Finance, Member of the European Parliament and European Commissioner for Agriculture and Rural Affairs. Now retired, he enjoys golf, fishing and racing, and is a member of the Turf Club. He maintains a keen interest in the Sligo Institute of Technology, for which he turned the first sod prior to its opening in 1970.

One Christmas Frank had a dozen to sell at Farniharpy on December 27, so on Stephen's Day he began walking them the 22 to 23 miles, in time to clean them up and have them looking good for the sale the next day. It began to snow.

The snow continued down in large, soft flakes quickly lying on the ground. Frank fell in with another man, Vincey Mullen, also taking a few to the fair. He put the cattle with Mrs McClout at 2d per head, and stayed the night at Mrs Irwan's

Frank at 17 with his sister Rose

for two shillings. When he woke next morning the snow lay three to four feet deep on the ground.

No one came to the fair to buy cattle. With snow like that, they would not know how long it would last and in particular whether they would have enough hay and fodder to sustain them through such a spell, even sup-posing they could have got there in the first place.

So there was Frank, stuck. He arranged to leave the cattle at the McClouts and set off to walk the 20 miles home. As he went, he called in to farmers along the way trying to book sales. He sold nine of them, all at a loss. Eventually, after about three to four weeks and the snow still thick on the ground he returned to Mrs McClout to settle up. He owed her more than the value of the three small calves that were left.

'It wasn't her fault, she and her husband had given them food and looked after them, so I paid her and came out onto the road and stood there, with twopence in my pocket. I was broke.'

He was in a dilemma. He was facing the trauma of having lost everything he had made so far. If he went home he would face the humiliating experience of telling his father he had gone bust. Should he go home and go to college, or continue as he was now?

It looked as if a thaw was starting. There was a fair due the next day in Ballina, another 25 miles on. Frank stood on the road and tossed a penny. It came down that he was to go to Ballina.

He took his time. He didn't want to arrive too early as he didn't have enough money for lodgings or even a cup of tea. Frank walked as slowly as he could through the night until 5.00 or 6.00 a.m. He began to be joined by other cattle men converging from all directions; the snow had lasted so long, and now everyone wanted to be at the fair. Frank fell in with a man with three small bullocks, asked him their price and bought them. He had no money to pay for them but he knew enough about the business to recognise value and to be sure he could sell them for a profit at the fair.

At the fair he met a man by the name of Paki (Patrick) O'Reilly from Enniskillen, who was in the export business; it was a propitious meeting. He wanted to buy Frank's recently acquired three cattle but Frank insisted on £1 a head profit instead of the usual five or ten shillings. This would be enormous for the time.

'I'll give you the money,' O'Reilly said.

Not only did he buy them, but he promptly commissioned Frank to buy more similar ones. 'This is a big fair gathering in and I have to buy big bullocks. You buy as many as you can just like those three if the price is similar, and I'll see you later.'

Frank could scarcely contain his delight. Once or twice during the day he met O'Reilly who expressed himself well pleased with Frank's purchases so far. By the end of the morning he had bought 97 head for O'Reilly.

'Make them up to 100,' O'Reilly said. He asked Frank to take them to the station for Belfast and to book them direct to himself. Frank had also bought a number for himself, and he needed to pay the men who had sold them to him. But O'Reilly hadn't yet paid him. What could he do?

On the rare days Frank wasn't at cattle fairs he was winning on the show jumping circuit and getting quite well known. He had his cheque book with him and went to the bank manager, Mr Lowry, in Ballina.

'He knew me and asked after the horses. I asked him for some money to buy the cattle and he said no problem at all, and put his mark on the cheque to enable me to withdraw money, even though my account in Sligo was empty.'

So Frank got enough money to pay for his cattle, then met O'Reilly having despatched them. He could have expected ten shillings a head as the norm for his work, but O'Reilly gave him all the luck pennies as well, which averaged five shillings a head.

'I had practically £100 for my morning's work which was very, very big.'

The first thing Frank did was get some belated breakfast – he hadn't eaten for two days – and then he decided to buy more cattle for himself.

He spent the afternoon buying some and selling them on again, repeating the process a number of times until in no time it was nearly dark, the fair was ending, and he found himself with five cattle on his hands, the buyers all gone, and he was nearly 40 miles from home.

He was advised to take them out to the nearby mill at Ard Na Ri. He stood them under the lights and as the men clocked off from the end of their day at the mill a number of them bought one or two of the cattle until all five were gone, at a profit.

'I'll never forget that day. I was really back on my feet again.'

The 40-mile walk home didn't worry him, no matter that he had walked all through the night before. He had earned in one day more than the money he had lost on the dozen cattle because of the snow and he was back in business.

From that day on he was a Dealer.

6

Dumped in the Clyde

Next morning Frank went straight into his bank in Sligo and lodged Paki O'Reilly's cheque for his work. He was ready to start up in export – and to keep on with the show jumping, which his cattle revenue subsidised.

From then on, Frank's routine would be to get up at 2.00 a.m. after three or four hours sleep, and drive perhaps 70 or 80 miles to a farm where he bought cattle. He would repeat the process over the next few days, arrange for the cattle to be shipped to England and then take the ferry and trains over himself to see them sold in the English markets.

'I was very rarely dry, seldom had a change of clothes, and was lucky if I got home once a month.'

He might have one long night's sleep and rest at home, and maybe get to a dance in the nearby barn, and then it was back to the same routine.

When he was twenty he briefly tried his hand at dealing in turkeys. It was 1967, the year of Foot and Mouth Disease.

He was asked by a chap called Neville Gilmour if he knew anything about buying turkeys and Frank said he did. They could be bought for two or three shillings a pound and sold for four shillings. Gilmour needed several loads before Christmas.

Frank on his 21st birthday

'Leave it to a fellow who knows,' Frank said blithely, and promptly found himself learning in detail the hard way about turkeys: that they mustn't have a crooked breast, or a full stomach, or a full craw on an empty stomach, and so on.

He went to the market at Tobercurry and bought a load of 300 to 400, put them into a big blue van and set off with Gilmour. It was at this point he discovered they were being smuggled across the Border, where they could fetch 5/- per pound.

Soon it was two vans and drivers, and Frank was buying up turkeys wherever he could – but as yet he hadn't received any money.

The next day the first of the two drivers was caught, and Gilmour decided it was too dangerous to transport the turkeys alive. They would have to be killed and plucked – that way they wouldn't make any noise in the lorry. Frank was paid for his first few loads, and then Gilmour told him he wanted him to buy cigarettes, which were rationed in the North.

On their next journey north, at the foot of a steep hill, they saw some police, and Neville nearly fainted for fear of not getting up the hill. He suggested turning back, but Frank wanted his money, and eventually they reached the smugglers' house where three or four were making tea.

When Frank was introduced one of them said, 'If you're a son of Jimmy McGarry you can't be a bastard.'

Slowly the money began coming in, but Frank had to go to many places to get it in dribs and drabs. It was not an enterprise he undertook again.

Frank McGarry makes the point that while a certain amount of luck can come into life success was really down to hard work.

'A fellow who used to get up late each morning told me I was lucky, but it was down to hard work, ingenuity and 18-hour days. You will have lucky breaks, but you will also have unlucky ones, but if your mind is made up and you want something badly enough you will get it, but you've got to work for it.'

From a young age Frank liked a good car. When he was about 18 he had a Baby Ford that had cost him £27. He was with a childhood friend, Mervy Hamilton, when they heard of two new Ford Tens for sale. Frank sold his Baby Ford for £55, but it still left him short of enough for the asking price.

A four-door unpainted grey model was up for £120 and the two-door £108 once painted; either would be reduced by £6 if left the basic grey. In the end they were offered two two-door models unpainted for £190, that is £95 each, plus two free number plates, tax and insurance for a year and a full tank of petrol. At the time the tax for a year cost £1.50 and the insurance was £1.00. Frank also bought a driving licence for two shillings!

As a young man Frank naturally did his share of courting, sometimes with more success than others. He remembers a time when in order to rendezvous with his date he had to get home from a cattle fair in England, taking the ferry and then three trains in order to meet the young lady in Sligo. Afterwards, he had to do all the travelling in reverse to get back to the UK.

Frank always liked a good car – here with his brothers John and Danny, Freddy McGettrick and friends from Galway

Frank tells an amusing story about the time he found himself with no clothes. He had done the usual runaround, buying cattle, and this time his last lot was from Ballinrobe. He wanted the 100 transported to England without any hanging around and so he had to hire and pay for the CIE lorry or private lorries in advance and hope to fill them. On this particular occasion the heavens opened while he was in Ballinrobe; it was 3.30 a.m. and the rain came down in stair-rods. As usual, the farmers he was buying from wanted paying in cash, although a number who knew him, and from whom he might be buying ten head at a time, were happy to take a cheque. The bank didn't open until 10.00 a.m. and Frank needed to be in Belfast to ensure all his cattle were boarded. Sometimes they would be 'outshipped', that is, he was told the ship was full and there was no room for them. In that case they would have to stay in yards at the docks with minimal feed. They could lose as much as a hundredweight overnight, and that was goodbye to his week's work and profit.

Frank was soaked through from the rain but he couldn't afford the time to stop in Sligo for a change of clothes, and headed straight for the ship. Once on board, with the cattle safely loaded, he visited the purser, Jimmy Treacy, who by this time knew him well; he could be assured of a good cabin and berth. He told him of his predicament of being wet through and no change of clothes for the next day's mart.

'Don't worry, leave them outside of the door and I'll see that they're hung by the furnace to dry,' the purser said.

At six the next morning the porter brought Frank a cup of tea, but no clothes; he looked blank when Frank asked for them. The purser was off duty and so the naked Frank lay in bed until at last the clothes were delivered – rolled up in the same wet and dirty ball that they had been in the night before. Apparently the porter who took them thought they were to be dumped. Not only were they still wet but they were crumpled, filthy dirty and stank. Frank had no alternative but to put them on, and head for the market at Forfar, clean up the cattle and do his best to sell them.

He says, 'I wasn't going to Forfar too often and the Irish at the time weren't regarded as the greatest or the cleanest people in the world. I always tried to hold my high esteem, I used to dress well and keep myself clean but that particular day I'm sure they thought, here's another Paddy with creased pants and creased coat, and creased waistcoat and the creased suit is filthy dirty and smelly.'

At a cattle mart in Forfar, Frank is second from the left

Frank went back on the boat that night and was straight into work the next day before going home, so still no change of clothes.

Frank's business grew and thrived. His first really big order came locally at Collooney Fair. He met a Welshman, John Strong, at dinner and the next day he showed him some of his cattle. They were too good for him as he only wanted little black Welsh heifers, but he agreed to a boatload of 50 as a sample. It was a huge order for Frank but before he went out to buy them he called on his bank manager, Sean Ford, because naturally he was concerned about paying for them before selling them on. Sean Ford showed his faith in the young man, as he was to on several occasions, and Frank bought the stock and shipped them.

Three weeks went by and he heard nothing. He didn't want to ring John Strong, but eventually he did.

Strong said, 'What cattle?'

That took Frank's breath away, and he was even more worried when he heard Strong had gone on a three-month Mediterranean cruise.

'I need to be paid for the cattle,' Frank said.

'Do you want money?'

'Of course I need some money.'

'Well, I only paid my last supplier at the end of the year. I will send you a cheque for the cattle, but there will be no more business from me.'

Apparently the previous dealer was so wealthy that he could wait for the money, and he would then add about £6 profit per head at the end of the year for the smaller cattle.

'Mine were better and I only charged £1 profit. It was my first really big order,' Frank says a little ruefully.

A much bigger hiccup was on its way.

It was 1952 and Frank was in his mid-twenties. Word came that English meat had come off rationing (still in place since WWII), and the population was crying out to eat beef. For many years they had been allowed only a matter of ounces per week. They were more used to corned beef hash, sausage made mostly from bread and salami-type meat.

Frank and another Irish dealer, Jimmy Cullen, decided to explore possibilities over there. It meant selling finished meat on the hook, that is, already killed, rather than as store cattle on the hoof (alive). It also meant buying over there, and a different type of animal. Frank was used to buying 70 head per week in Ireland, maybe 100 with the help of the bank, but now a new skill was called upon.

'We had to know the business to a halfpenny in a pound. We purchased them by the hundredweight, and you had to tell the weight of the animal by looking.'

The two men stayed in the White Swan Hotel in Alnwick, Northumberland, bought a number of suitable beasts, had them killed in Glasgow and then took them to Belgrove Market, Glasgow. It was a whole different way of selling, because instead of it being a live animal it was a carcase on a hook. At first, all went well, because the demand was so great. Frank and Jimmy were staying in the Caledonian Hotel in Edinburgh, Claridges in London when they were supplying Smithfield and the North British in Glasgow.

'We had to stay in the best hotels because that was the only time we got a sleep, a shower and clean up and good food, because the restaurants at that time all had terrible food.'

They soon found they were making profits of about 60 per cent. They got braver and bought more. The price they had to pay was rising but they kept selling for good profit. They were buying in markets like Alnwick, Berwick upon Tweed and Woller, and selling them in Smithfield, Edinburgh and Glasgow.

'If you wanted them killed and got in at the right time in the market, you had to tip the fellow in the abattoir, and if you wanted a good price for the livers you had to tip the fellow that was selling them and he'd get you a good price. It was the same with the hides, and with your agent if you had one.'

The prices they were buying at steadily began to rise, almost without them noticing.

'We bought anyway and we were getting braver because we were getting so much profit.'

Frank bought up to 100 a time and Jimmy, a wealthy man, would buy 300.

'We were doing so well because they were very easy to sell, and we had especially good ones; the butchers were mad looking for them. We were doing great and we couldn't get enough at this stage.'

This went on for seven or eight weeks of going so hard they had barely a spare minute. They were running from market to market, eating and sleeping on trains and drinking tea at the market cafes, and they were making a fortune.

One day Frank walked into the four-acre Bellgrove Market site in Glasgow as usual, ready to sell his 300 beasts; the 600 sides were already hanging from hooks. There were no buyers there. The boom had gone bust. The buying price had gone up to £11 (from the original £3, and up in one shilling increments). It seemed that the people had had their fill of beef and were replete.

It was serious. Occasionally a butcher would come along and select a couple of fillet steaks from one carcase, and pick out the ribs from another. In desperation Frank would sell them, but the rest of the carcasses began to go off. Before long they stank. The Corporation intervened and ordered their removal, but there was nowhere for them to go. People didn't have fridges, let alone deep freezers, in those days. It seems unthinkable today, but the solution was that they were dumped into the Clyde.

Frank was devastated. He couldn't bear to be there when it was done, and never spoke of it again. Once more, he was broke. Everything was lost in those dumped cattle. Jimmy went back to Ireland and asked if Frank was coming with him.

'No, I'm not going back a loser.'

'What are you going to do here?'

'I don't know, but I've got to do something. Maybe I'll clean the streets – and I certainly won't be staying in this smart hotel, I'll have to find somewhere cheap.'

So the two men parted on the Glasgow street, Jimmy first lending Frank £10. That was the only money Frank had. He found bed and breakfast digs with a woman called Mrs Chisholm and gave her £3 for two weeks.

He headed for Alnwick to see if he could get a job hosing the cattle yards. The manager Matt Young greeted him warmly.

'There's been a complete flop in the market since you were last here, what are you buying?'

Frank explained his sorry situation and offered to sweep the yards at £1/10- a week. Matt Young wouldn't hear of it.

'Buy some cattle, put them down to me, and pay me when you've sold them,' he said.

Once in the ring, with beautiful quality coming in at knock down prices, Frank couldn't resist the dealer in him. He bought 17 and says it would have been more if he had had the guts. He took them to Glasgow but the butchers there were in for a surprise. He refused to sell them dead.

'Nobody will buy them,' one butcher told him.

'Sure, well, then I can put them in a field with hay. There's no more killing for me and there's nobody ever again going to dump my cattle in the Clyde. I'm never selling them on the hook again.'

One butcher said, 'No one will buy them that way.'

'Then they'll have to do without them,' Frank said, 'that's the change there's going to be.'

Frank installed his cattle in separate pens around the market place. He recognised a small Jewish butcher who used to demand one fillet out of one carcase and two sirloins out of another.

Now he said, 'I want some meat.'

Frank told him his cattle were all promised.

'My shop will have to close, I haven't a beast.'

Frank had one small beast there that he had bought for £3 per hundredweight. He told the butcher he could have it for £15 per hundredweight.

'You must be mad. They're not making more than £4.'

'Don't worry, there's plenty of other butchers mad looking for them. I only have 17 in the market and they are the only animals here.'

He ended up selling the man two for £15 per hundredweight. Word spread round the market that both men were crazy. Frank told other butchers, 'I'm going to remain crazy. There are only 15 left, and if I don't get £15 per hundredweight I'm not selling one.'

They were all sold – and Frank went back to Alnwick with money in his pockets again. It was the last time that he hit the floor.

Not that he rested on his laurels.

7

Cattle King

Frank's first stop was to pay back his debt to Matt Young in Alnwick, and then it was about two months of pure roller-coaster, travelling between markets buying at one and selling at another. He never slept in a bed let alone a hotel in that time, taking what sleep and food, and even washing, that he could on the trains between markets, accompanied by a bag with spare clothes, the money he was accumulating, and nothing else.

Eventually, after about nine weeks, he returned to Mrs Chisholm, whose digs he had spent not a single night in.

'What's happened to you?' she looked aghast at the sight of him.

'I'm very busy.'

'I'll tell you, you're going to die. Let me give you a drink.'

'I don't drink.'

'Well, you'll just have to,' Mrs Chisholm said, 'because I think you're going to die, and I'll get you something to eat, and I'll put a hot water bottle in your bed, and you go and try and sleep.'

'I haven't been in a bed since I last saw you.'

'You look like it.'

He had lost a stone in weight.

So Frank had what was then a rare drink, asked to be called in time for Mass in the morning, and went to bed. When he woke up, he dressed ready for Mass. Mrs Chisholm asked him where he was going, and he told her.

'It's Monday, not Sunday,' she said. 'You slept all day yesterday and I didn't call you.'

Frank immediately changed and headed back for the market. There he met Frank Bachelor who asked Frank if he could buy cattle as good in Ireland as he had in England he would like Frank to buy for him. It was the start of the big time in the cattle dealing world.

He returned to Sligo, lodged his money, and began buying store cattle not only for Frank Bachelor but for many others. A sign of the times was that he could arrive in Dublin at 2.30 a.m. and leave his car in Annamo Garage on Hanlans Corner, Cabra, where it would be filled with petrol; a full tank cost £1. More than that, he would leave a note requesting the car to be valeted. He would leave it unlocked not only with his various belongings in it, but both the glove box and a bag stashed with cash would also be inside. He would return in the afternoon to a clean car and everything still safely inside it.

Not that the car was always clean. He was driving about 2,000 miles a week and so it would frequently be covered in dust. He tells the story of one time when he was driving in Dublin and found himself in the wrong lane. A policeman raised his hand to stop him and was about to admonish him when he peered into the old Mercedes. The inside of the car was covered in old coats and hats, muddy boots and nearly as much dust as clung to the outside of the car.

'Up from the bog, I suppose?' the policeman asked.

'Yes, do you want a seat home?' Frank replied.

In his early days of cattle dealing Frank would try to find the cheapest overnight accommodation possible. It was quite normal in those days not only to share a room with a total stranger but also a bed. There was one particular time when a storm blew up and on reaching Belmullet the only hotel was full. There were three in the bed that particular night and one man, Jimmy, when he wanted to turn over would say, 'will ye lie spoons,' and the three men all turned over, tucked together like spoons.

Sometimes there were five in a bed, and Frank might not know the other four. Such digs would cost about 2/6d (12 and a half pence) a night.

In about the early 1950s Frank travelled to France, a journey that took three days by train and a ferry from Ireland to England and then on to France. Under Irish law at the time he was allowed to take a maximum of £30 out of the country. His intention was to obtain a contract for supplying the American forces in Germany and a meeting was set up in Paris. He secured a contract for a weekly boatload of heavy cattle, which were unpopular in Ireland at the time.

The next time he was in the Dublin mart he bought some big cattle from another well-known cattleman, Jack Keogh, and his son Raymond. They wondered why he wanted them. At first Frank was reluctant to say, but once he told them – adding that the Americans would like two loads a week but Frank couldn't afford that – the Keoghs came in with him, Frank covering the west, and the Keoghs the south and east. Frank was to meet Raymond Keogh again some 60 years later at Tommy Brennan's funeral in 2014.

On another occasion when he was in Europe Frank learnt of an international show not too far away and took himself off to it, in the sixpenny enclosure, the grandstand being a future dream. There, the Irishman Colonel Dan Corry was chef d'equipe (Frank believes) when one of the Irish riders, Roger Moloney, broke his leg shortly before he was due to ride in the main competition, the Nations Cup. The story goes that as the ambulance was about to drive off with the injured rider Colonel Corry halted it, went inside and took the breeches, boots and tunic off Moloney and put them on himself. He hadn't competed for a few years, but he then went out and got on Moloney's horse, which he had never ridden before, and proceeded to jump two impeccable clear rounds.

It was the sort of occasion that further fired Frank's childhood dream of show jumping, or at least being involved in it. Dan Corry had been a lynchpin of the (all military) show jumping team since 1928 (Dublin) right through until after WWII. He was on the winning Nations Cup teams in Lucerne in 1931; Boston, 1932; Toronto 1933; Lucerne, Dublin and New York in 1935; Nice, Amsterdam, Lucerne and Dublin in 1936; another three in 1937 including on home territory in Dublin; and an amazing Nice, Dublin, New York and Toronto in 1938. After World War II Dan Corry was still there on winning teams: Dublin in 1946 and 1949, as well as Harrisburg that year.

In the cattle business it was more important than anything else to have a good name with the banks. Frank would obtain advices (notes granting credit) from his bank manager in Shop Street, Eyre Square, Galway, on most fair days to be used at such places as Ballina, Ballinrobe, Tuam, Swinford, Galway, Headford, Loughrea, Athenry, Gort and so on.

'If anything went wrong with any of your cheques you could say goodbye to your business,' Frank says.

Frank began stocking stud farms with the little black Aberdeen Angus store cattle with which he was earning a good reputa-

*Some of Frank's trademark Aberdeen Angus
cattle (no ear tags in those days)*

tion. One such was John Bellingham from County Westmeath, who had 32 farms in all.

Frank would sell them to customers but guarantee to buy them back. That way Frank got them grazed, the stud and land owners made some money – and Frank made more.

Rockwell College and Terenure College were two of his clients, and another was Curragh trainer Paddy Prendergast.

It was after Frank bought them back that they were usually exported to England and Scotland where they were fattened up and finished off for beef.

One time he sent a load at £60 per head to Willie Nesbit in Northumberland. Nesbit rang to say they weren't of the quality that he usually received from him. Frank immediately said he would take them back but, because of travel restrictions, they had to stay on Nesbit's land for a while; it was May when the grass was growing. As soon as he could, Frank collected them and booked them into a fair where the top bunch made £66. When it came to the least good lot it was Nesbit himself who bought them for £63.

He met Frank and laughed. 'Never again will I return any animal to you – in future I'll order all my cattle from you.'

Frank says, 'It was a case of don't let a pimple fester. I nipped it in the bud by immediately agreeing to take the cattle back rather than arguing.'

Frank always attended the Smithfield Christmas fair and show where he more than once won the carcase competition. He won similar competitions at Edinburgh and Glasgow with his trademark Aberdeen Angus. He would also pick out show cattle for Alex Stubbor with which to go on and win the Smithfield Fatstock show. One time he picked out a small calf from among the bullocks and told a surprised Alex that that was the one. Frank had intended it for when it was a carcase but six months later Alex Stubbor rang him to say he had won the live Smithfield Championships with it.

In later years, two heifers that Frank sold to Mr Hetherington went on to be champion and reserve in Perth, Scotland.

Frank was still in his early twenties and buying for his older brother John. One time he brought home just over 100 head of cattle from Boyle Fair and put them in a field. Next day John came to see them and was not pleased. He said they were too expensive and that he would lose a fortune.

'He gave me a hell of a drubbing, but he was a great teacher. He even commented that I was wearing the wrong colour socks – they were white.'

Frank was still feeling upset when he met up with nine or ten other dealers in Maddens, Collooney, and had Sunday lunch there, something he never got at a fair.

Emboldened, he went to John and said, 'I was man enough to buy them, and I will be man enough to sell them.'

He booked a train for them to Northallerton, Yorkshire, via the ferry to Stranraer, but when he got there not a single man

*Perth Mart Harvest Show, late 1990s – Frank won champion
heifer – left is Mr Hetherington, right is Jimmy Brays, both
customers of Frank's*

would give him a penny for the beasts. At length a nice man
came over to him, and explained that they were the wrong cattle for that particular place, but suggested he take them to York
the following Thursday where they liked to buy good cattle like
Frank's.

As Frank discovered, 'You don't go to Goffs for a cob,' it's
more a question of 'horses for courses.'

Frank took them to York, penned them up and was cleaning them early on the market morning when a police car drove
up and stopped by him.

'Are you Frank McGarry?'

'Yes.'

'Come with us.'

Frank knew nothing about England and didn't know what
was wrong. He soon discovered. He should have had a licence
to bring the cattle over, and without it they had been moved

illegally. He could be held in detention for seven days. Luckily, the sergeant believed the young man and let him off.

'So, being cheeky, I asked to be taken back to the market in the police car.'

Once there, he said, 'Do me a favour, please. These people will think I'm a criminal. Will you come to the auctioneer and announce why you held me.'

Everyone gathered round, and the sergeant explained that the young Irishman had made a mistake and that he was 100 per cent honest.

'I did the best trade; they bought my cattle like hot cakes. I got about £3 a head profit, and my brother had said they'd make a loss of £5 per head.'

In time, Frank and other cattle dealers began encountering increasing problems with shipping cattle out from Dublin. All too often, if Frank took 100 head for shipping, only 80 or sometimes as few as 50 would go. The rest were held up in a pen on the North Wall. The week's work was ruined, and it became apparent that those supplying 'brown envelopes' to the workers were the ones whose cattle went.

'The fella with the biggest back-hander got the most cattle away,' says Frank.

At last he went to the office, and said, 'If you don't get all my animals away I'll leave the grass growing on the quay.'

He says now, 'It was a big statement from a little fella to a very big firm.'

He didn't get all his cattle away and the result was he and a number of others from the West formed a company called the Western Livestock Exporters Company. They sold about 200 shares in it to people within the trade only, and ten directors were appointed with Frank, in spite of his youth, as chairman.

They decided they would buy a boat themselves and start shipping from Sligo. It would be a long way round the north coast of Ireland to Glasgow, but they worked out a cost effective figure of £3 per head which would be highly competitive with the big Dublin company. Bed linen and drink would be provided for the men accompanying the stock. The idea would also bring increased business for local farmers and traders in terms of hay, dock work and so forth.

It was not straight forward. For one thing, Sligo harbour had silted up and needed dredging, and for another, a large capital sum of money would need to be found to buy a ship, obtain lairage (holding pens), and recruit and pay the staff. But Frank had the bit between his teeth.

'Luckily, Charlie Haughey was Minister for Agriculture at the time,' Frank recalls, 'and he approved a grant of £7,000 for dredging the tidal harbour and for providing lairage. It was a big sum at the time.'

While getting these tasks accomplished the WLE company was looking for a suitable ship. One night Frank's bank manager Sean Ford rang him. It was 1.00 a.m. and he asked Frank to come down to the hotel they were in right away to meet two men, a Captain Brady and local timber businessman James Kiernan, who was trying to help the company.

'If they're good or bad I can see them in the morning,' Frank said.

At 9.00 a.m. he met them at the hotel. They seemed very plausible and Captain Brady had supposedly been awarded a medal by President Kennedy in the Cuban missile crisis.

One of the decisions the company had to make was whether to go for a small ship that could cope with low tide or a bigger one which would have tidal restraints, but could obviously carry more stock. Frank told the two men his requirements, and they told him they had a boat that suited him in every respect. It was an ex-troop carrier, available with cattle pens already on it.

'It was so accurate that I felt worried,' he says, 'but I called a directors' meeting and the decision was to go ahead.'

Frank met the men in the Imperial Hotel, Sligo, along with Sean Ford, and handed over a cheque for £40,000 deposit on the £180,000 ship.

On reflection he felt uneasy about the deal; some inner sense told him it was too good to be true. He called another directors' meeting and said he felt suspicious; he was afraid this could be a bogey man. He rang the bank to stop the cheque. Sean Ford, the manager, did so, but was not happy and said he would get a bank report on Captain Brady.

Back came a glowing report. Brady had property and trees in the Amazon, and appeared a sound prospect (all bogus, it subsequently transpired).

Frank, feeling contrite, apologised for stopping the cheque. Brady was cross with him but agreed to meet. Once more, the businessman was very convincing but said he would not accept a cheque again. If the deal was to be re-opened it would be cash only. Frank duly paid up on behalf of the company.

The promised boat did not turn up. Frank waited – and waited, and waited.

'I knew we'd been done,' he says. 'I went to the company's solicitor, Bernard Brennan – he's a judge now – and Brady agreed to meet us in the Intercontinental Hotel, now Jury's, in Dublin Four.'

At the meeting, attended by five members of the company, and Brady, Kiernan and their entourage, Frank McGarry stunned them by announcing he wanted to buy a bigger boat.

'It will cost you more,' Brady said.

'That doesn't matter,' Frank replied.

One of the directors, aghast, kicked him under the table.

'I'll take an order,' Brady said.

Frank said, 'I have a lot of shareholders, about 200, and they just don't trust you now, and they will ask me explicitly about it. You said you would reimburse us if we have any problems – do we still have a deal?'

The man agreed.

'I have a contract here,' Frank said, and pulled it from his pocket and read it to them, and Kiernan and Brady signed it.

So Frank had thereby achieved his objective of getting the men's signatures on a contract. Subsequently, the company took Kiernan to court and got 60 per cent of their original outlay back.

Frank says, 'Brady had done a runner and Kiernan was a gentleman and it was most unfortunate that he got involved, when trying to help.'

Meanwhile, of course, the company still had no boat, so they hired one from Monsieur Beauclair from Belgium, and it sailed out of Sligo for many years.

'It was an absolute success,' Frank says.

The route only came to an end following a dockers' strike. The company had to hire 13 dockers who were not used to handling animals. Until that point, the company had been an unmitigated success. They had taken on the big boys and beaten them to both sides' surprise.

Frank says, 'And so we did leave the grass growing on the Quay, and eventually there were no cattle at all being shipped out of Dublin.'

There was an auction one time of the contents of the Ursuline Convent in Sligo, to be followed by the sale of land which Frank was interested in. A character called Harry McGowan was auctioneer and as Frank arrived he heard a lot knocked down to him. It turned out to be a quantity of about 30 school desks for £2. The auctioneer had no bids and told Frank when he saw him he thought they would make good jumps. In fact, with their iron legs, they would be potentially dangerous for that purpose, but another man then came along wanting four desks and bought them off Frank for £10. He did buy church pews at another auction and faced them back to back to make jumps.

Before the land came up Frank was approached by a man badly wanting to buy it. Correctly identifying Frank as his likely rival he asked him not to bid, and so Frank agreed. He was well able to buy useful plots of land, as we shall see.

In 1974 the Irish Government put an embargo on the export of in-calf heifers. It was afraid that so many were going to England that Ireland's gene pool was in danger.

Frank was convinced something would go wrong with such a stricture. This was January and he considered that come autumn the prices would drop dramatically if there was no export market. He rang a friend in Scotland, Ron Mattes, and asked him to find a shed and silage for 350 head. He then sent over his 350 in-calf blue heifers, beating the ban by a matter of days. Next, he put his land into hay and didn't buy any cattle, something that was alien to him. The cattle prices that were given out on the radio every evening were getting worse and worse, and all the talk was about how bad the situation was. Frank made hay and put it in his cattle sheds.

Peter Eckert, head of a German riding school in Wiesbaden, rang wanting five horses. The party came over for a week and were plied with *poitín*, food and drink every night. The prices were to be given in Deutschmarks and the men had brought bank drafts over with them. It was early October and when the five horses had gone, Frank decided to visit the mart at Ballymoate, 'just for a look'.

'Take your cheque book,' his wife Noreen said. 'I know you.'

To the surprise of all around him, he soon began buying cattle. First, he bought three from a friend, but as the sale prices kept going down and down he kept buying, ending up with 78 at that sale.

Frank's brother, John, pulled him to one side. 'What's gone wrong with you? You're buying! You're mad!'

'Before you chastise me, come and have a look,' Frank said.

He showed him a fine bunch of cattle that had cost him £29 a head, instead of the £250 to 300 each that could normally have been expected.

'If they go any lower than that there won't be any farms left,' Frank said.

He then made a conscious decision that he couldn't afford to keep his horses in. He closed the riding school and turned all 20 horses out, unclipped, on Coney Island, where their long coats and the sand dunes would protect them during winter.

One of the Irish estates he used to supply with cattle was Lord Carew at Castletown in County Kildare.

To the relief of Lord Carew, who had heard of the cattle disaster, Frank said he did not propose selling him any cattle that winter. He asked if he could rent his land instead and Lord Carew was delighted to agree.

It was now the end of November and Frank had bought a great many head of cattle, a large number of which he despatched to Castletown. He also had 350 in his own sheds, and 80 in the stables (with six to a stable).

When it came to the marts the following autumn it was Frank who had cattle to sell when virtually no one else had. Once more, he had read the market and had the foresight – and bravery – to stock up, and was able to meet the supply and demand, attaining excellent prices.

8

Early Show Jumping

Frank got into a good routine and as his reputation (and bank balance) grew, so he found he could indulge in his passion for show jumping in June, July and August, which coincided with the quiet period for the cattle dealing. He was living in Sligo town, and rented stables firstly from a chemist, whose daughter, Hilda Togher, became Frank's jockey, usually riding in Style and Appearance classes, winning lots of classes with a nearly black mare called Dark Rosaleen.

Frank was later to rent a yard from Paddy Kilgallon in the Sligo Mall, and then Andy Dodd's yard until his eventual move to his own Carrowmore, of which more later.

In those days, the show jumping season began with Banbridge in County Down, Northern Ireland on Easter Monday, and ended with Ballinasloe, County Galway, in the first week of October, after which Frank would dash home to try to see the Horse of the Year Show in Harringay, London on his black and white TV.

The year's highlight was the RDS show at Ballsbridge, Dublin in August; there were no winter shows. Show jumping began at the RDS in its first annual horse show 1868 with a 'Leaping Competition', after initial trial shows in 1864 and 1866. It was well advertised and held on the lawn of Leinster House, now home to the Dáil, Ireland's parliament. Just one separate fence was jumped on each of the four days, and only those who cleared the first day's fence could proceed to the next day, and so on, until the final on day four. (Britain did not start 'lepping' contests until fifteen years later.)

The prizes for the high and wide leaps were £5 for first and £2 for second with £10 and a cup to the winner of the championship and a riding crop and a fiver to the runner-up. The crowds flocked in.

The fence on day one was described as the 'High Leap' and was of timber, four feet, six inches high, trimmed with gorse. Day two was the wide leap – twelve feet of water faced by gorse-filled timber. Day three was the stone wall, comprised of loose stones rising to a narrower top. Rumour had it that for the final on day four it was six feet high, and some 6,000 spectators filled the lawn to watch the nine finalists who had come through from day three. It was won by Richard Flynn, a Strokestown, County Roscommon sheep farmer, with his horse Shaun Rue.

Shaun Rue was sold to Tom Conolly of Castletown, County Kildare for the enormous sum of £1,000 (roughly equivalent to £0.5 million today), and he hunted him. Ninety-eight years later, in 1966, Tom's great-granddaughter Diana Conolly-Carew won the main RDS show jumping event, the International Grand Prix, with Barrymore, so Castletown was once more home to Ireland's champion show jumper.

The show moved to its current Ballsbridge, Dublin home in 1881. 'Prize jumping' for high jump and long jump became an equestrian discipline at the 1900 Olympic Games in Paris, the second games of the modern Olympiad and the first in which women were allowed to compete, but it was not until the 1912

Stockholm Olympics that a Nations Cup-style show jumping event was staged.

The Banbridge show catalogue cost 2/6d. Frank found one in a pocket of an old coat that he gave to a chap for an amateur dramatic play. The cost of entry for the grand prix show jumping class was 5/- for a £15 prize.

The season was almost exclusively outdoors, with just one show held indoors. This was Burton Hall, Stillorgan, Dublin, close to Leopardstown racecourse and owned by Colonel Joe Hume-Dugeon. (It is now owned by Dublin County Council and used as a day care centre.)

'Colonel Dugeon was a grand old man who never shod his horses,' says Frank.

Frank's time in the saddle proved limited due to his business, but his prowess lay in work on the ground and in management.

He says, 'Getting a horse to a fence is more important than the jumping. Jumping only takes a moment but getting to a fence takes a number of seconds.'

So he gave his horses plenty of work on the flat, and was probably ahead of his time in this respect. He had that inherent stockman's eye, be it for beast or horse or man, and an ability to work with nature. It was from this time that he started bringing on promising young riders, tutoring them in his way. He also built up a reputation for being good with mares (they can tend to be temperamental), and he would not work them when they were in season.

From the time of Rock Prince, the pony who went to the Duke and Duchess of Norfolk for their daughter Sarah Howard, Frank was hooked on show jumping, and was seldom without one or two thereafter. Just how much he did for Irish show jumping will become apparent.

Throughout his cattle export days he had been quietly competing with his show jumpers, whenever he had the time. Rock Prince set the ball rolling as we have seen, and after him came a pony called The Brat. He stood 13.2 hands high (138 centimetres) and yet he was able to jump five feet, ten inches in height – with four inches to a hand, that was much higher than the four feet, six inches of The Brat's height.

Frank had watched him at a number of local shows and could see that he was exceptional. He wasn't particularly good looking but he would jump as successfully against horses as he did ponies. In those days, there was no show jumping association in Ireland, and so there were no rules and regulations, meaning that The Brat could jump in any class.

Frank bought him off Willie Hughes in Cashel Connor in Sligo and asked his regular rider, John Rowe from Ballina, to continue riding him. (John's father, Paddy Rowe, owned Loch Conn who finished second to Caughoo in the 1947 Grand National at Aintree.) Frank paid £100, a figure that people in the countryside generally considered no pony could possibly be worth, especially for a comparatively green pony with only a few shows under his belt.

Frank had won a particular class at Sligo Show for the last two years and was keen to win it a third time which would result in him keeping the cup. Unfortunately, The Brat's lack of experience told because there was a bank, an obstacle he had not encountered before. The Brat hit the top of it and turned over, breaking John's arm in the process.

Frank says, 'John Rowe is a lovely guy and still a friend.'

After that show, The Brat teamed up firstly with Seamus Gilmartin, and was prepared by Hilda Togher, and he would jump in every competition at a show, winning most of them. At one, he won the 13.2, the 14.2, another one after that, and then the high jump, at which point Frank arrived on the scene, having been out buying cattle. The little pony had five rosettes, but then there was a drag hunt, the first home to be the winner, and he won that as well, beating horses as well as bigger ponies.

One year Frank took him to the popular Spring Show in Dublin, now defunct, and by this time Francie Kerins had begun what was to be a 17-year association riding for Frank. It was there that John Bernard McNicholl from the North tried desperately to buy the little star for his sons Brian and Peter.

Frank takes up the story. 'They had a couple of good ponies in the North, and that was a much hotter place to jump in at the time than the free state. We used to compete there when we wanted to know how good our horses were. John wanted to buy the pony and I didn't want to sell him. Eventually he bid me more than the pony was worth, and I said I'd sell a half share in him.'

McNicholl agreed on condition that the pony could jump in his name. He was ridden in the North's flagship show, Balmoral, by Willie Rooney's daughter, Ann (now Ferris; both she and her sister, Rosemary became top amateur race riders). The Queen was present (it was 1953 and her Coronation year) and Frank had a picture of her standing beside a huge fence when she presented Ann Rooney with the cup. Soon after, Frank offered McNicholl his half share for nothing on condition he didn't sell the pony.

After the ponies, Frank gradually moved up to horses.

One of Frank's early helpers was schoolgirl Monica Cleave (now Flanagan) who went on to a life in horses, mostly abroad, and then became a local Grand Prix photographer. Monica remembers:

According to Frank McGarry I am the only woman who ever made him cry, and I did so at the age of 16 in 1961. He bought a big bay horse called Big John and because he had no stable empty to put him in he asked my mother if he could be stabled with us for a short while. My mother agreed and the horse arrived. Our yard had one large loose box and six straight stalls. My horse was in the loose box so it stood to reason that Big John would be in one of the stalls. So he wouldn't be lonely, I put him in the stall next my horse who had easy access to his rump. I didn't know he ate tails but I soon found out and so did Frank – hence the tears. Frank's horse was going to the Dublin Horse Show a few days later and was to be ridden by Lady Hemphill. Frank stood around wringing his hands and crying while I stood in silence quite unable to speak for the shame of it all. But then Frank had an idea. He came back with a tail taken, so he said, from a dead horse. He stuck it on in clumps with some sort of glue and the horse went off to Dublin. Never in all my born days will I forget watching Big John doing a fine extended trot down the long side of the ring with Lady Hemphill looking radiant while lumps of tail hair wafted off his tail and into the spectator area. I can laugh now, and so can Frank, but I never got over the shame of it. Jos Masters was very keen to buy the horse after the class and Frank left it until the closing minutes of the deal to tell him of the eaten tail. The ending was good because Jos wanted the horse no matter what was spoiling his beauty.

That same summer was one of the very best of my teenage summers. I travelled the country with Francie Kerins, Cecil Mahon and the three grey geldings – Go-Sly-Up, Dooney Rock and Smokey Joe. At that time Frank had a very black-smoky Land Rover with a soft top and a three-horse box. When the horses were loaded and the

Monica Cleave on Menzies

*three of us in the Land Rover there was very little room
left for much else so Frank would drive to the shows in
his car with all the tack in the boot. Once, at Lousiburgh
Show in the extreme west of County Mayo, a local happened to look into the boot and exclaimed to his compan-
ion that he'd never seen 'so many straps and buckles' in
his life. Those three horses won between them all before
them. I used to be allowed to ride one of them into the
ring to collect his ribbon at presentation-time and I'd
be proud as punch. At one notable time we crossed over
the border into Northern Ireland and back on fourteen
consecutive days.*

*I loved Go-Sly-Up because of his honesty and his brav-
ery and his wit, but I adored Smokey Joe. Frank used to
hunt him in the winter but on one lucky day I rode the
horse to the meet for him and he didn't turn up, so Francie said I could hunt him myself. He was a Rolls Royce
compared to anything I had hunted up to then and I still*

remember the thrill of him springing over walls with an elasticity to die for.

Another horse of Frank's that I enjoyed was Menzies. I don't think he showjumped all that well, otherwise I would never have been given him to show in hunter classes! My only claim to fame with him was that I won the hunters on him at Sligo Show. Being from Sligo made the win ever so special and I was quite a star in school after the summer holidays.

Another friendship that has lasted more than 60 years was with Lady Perdita Blackwood, for whom Frank originally found a pony via his cousin Patsy Gilmartin, brother of Seamus. He later became a judge at her shows, penned a poem for her 70th birthday and more recently attended her 80th birthday party.

There was a time when Frank was on a rare holiday, in the Isle of Man, with no cattle or horse-dealing on the agenda – or so he thought. He ran short of money, went into a bank in Douglas and spoke to the bank manager, a Mr Almond, to ask if he would take a cheque, after he had had a couple of days to check with his bank in Sligo.

'Ah, you've an honest enough face, I'll give you the money.'

They chatted for a while, and Mr Almond said, 'Ireland's supposed to be a great horsey country.'

'Oh, it is, of course.'

'My daughter's a show jumper, here in the Isle of Man, I've a notion of going to Ireland to buy her a horse.'

Frank gave him his address, took the money and continued with his holiday, not thinking of the matter again.

Soon after he was home there was a knock on his door and he found a good looking girl of about 17 standing there. She introduced herself as Valerie Almond. It didn't ring any bell

Lady Perdita Blackwood, 1965, with arab stallion Dominic, in step

with Frank until she added that she came from the Isle of Man. Frank directed them down to the Southern Hotel in Sligo and said he would meet them for dinner.

After a shower and change he looked considerably more respectable. Frank's eyes had been taken by the girl, but he soon found she was well-minded by her father, and was in the middle, inaccessible room of their suite!

Next day they saw a couple of horses and bought one. Valerie asked to see Frank's own horses, but he had nothing good enough at the time. She insisted, and fell for a dark mare. Frank told her it would not make a jumper, but could win a show class or be a hunter.

They bought it because, Frank believes, 'she wanted some sort of souvenir of mine'. At a price of £250, it was also a good profit for him.

But there was just one horse Frank had in his long career that was never going to be sold, no matter what the offer.

9

The Horse Who Couldn't Stop Winning

One Sunday in 1954 Frank arrived at Enniscrone show just as the jumping classes had finished. He was approached by a man called Jack Ormsby who told him he had missed seeing a small horse with an exceptionally big jump. They went and found his owner, one John Ray, and watched the little grey horse ridden without a saddle or bridle. With only a piece of rope around his head he cantered down the Champion Walk where the fences in the now deserted ring stood at more than five feet.

Frank was itching to buy him but he had a firm rule about not dealing on the Sabbath, so first thing on Monday morning he sought the owner again. He bought the little horse for the asking price of £75, less £3 luck money. If he had been prepared to buy on a Sunday the price would have been £40 but by Monday a number of other people had expressed their interest.

Until that time the little horse's career had mainly consisted of hauling telegraph poles as electrification was brought to the west of Ireland. Apparently when the workers had finished in the evening the fellow working for John Ray rode the horse straight back across country, bareback and with no bridle, jumping whatever fences crossed their path and not bothering with going on any roads, including the telegraph poles lying on the ground waiting for erection.

Nothing and no one, not even a prophet, could have foreseen that this little cob would become the winningest show jumper in Irish history, and probably the world – then and now. From the start he was a gentle horse who also became a huge character at home; he was also very strong. Because he had had no formal training, Frank was able to mould him to his way, and within a week or two of buying him, he took him to his first show, at Belturbet in County Cavan. There, ridden by Francie Kerins, he won the two classes he contested.

Francie Kerins on Go-Sly-Up with Lough Gill on the left and Sligo Bay on the right, 1954

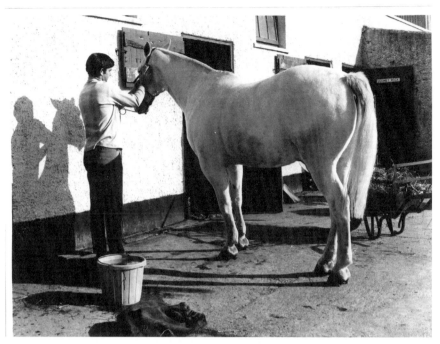

Groom Cecil Mahon was devoted to Go-Sly-Up

Frank registered his name as Go-Sly-Up, Up Sligo in reverse, the first of the many horses that subsequently bore his
home county's name. Frank's groom Cecil Mahon nicknamed
him Dandy and built up an exceptional rapport with him over
the years. Cecil and Frankie both joined Frank at the age of 16.
Cecil stayed with him for about 17 years plus as a schoolboy
and Frankie also for about 17 years, the two of them overlap-
ping for a number of years, and Cecil also won a number of
jumping classes on the little horse. Cecil also competed on an
aptly-named mare, Speedy Star, which he rode once he was
good enough and after Francie had enough other horses to
ride.

Standing just 15.1 hands high and with his modest breeding – by 'Nothing' out of 'Nothing' – big things were not expected of Go-Sly-Up, yet eleven years later he had won 513 first
prizes in show jumping at shows; the previous national record

was 22. This was before there were timed jump-offs, and so he might have to jump as many as six rounds until he was 'the last man standing'.

Frank says, 'He had little if any pure blood in him and other people considered him probably the plainest horse I ever owned or jumped, but there was something very likeable about him and he was a grand type of cob.'

So to prove them wrong Frank took him to Dublin show and promptly won the cob class.

He was by the same sire as The Brat, whose owner Willie Hughes said had very little breeding at all. His progeny from ordinary mares were all good jumpers, so if he had been put to thoroughbred or three-quarter-bred mares the results could have been phenomenal.

'My father used to say "an ounce of breeding is worth ten tons of feeding",' Frank recalls, yet from the first Go-Sly-Up was a star in the making. He jumped for eleven seasons, from 1955 to 1966, and after his first season he had already reached Grade A and was mostly jumping in Grand Prix and puissance (high jump), the highest grade of show jumping over the most challenging tracks. It was this precocity that led Frank into making a rare mistake: he let his youngster go to the RDS Dublin Show in Ballsbridge, Ireland's annual showcase every August of the very best of Irish show horses and ponies, and show jumpers.

Go-Sly-Up was over-faced and stopped, something that became virtually unknown in his life. In the puissance wall horses were allowed up to two stops, but Go-Sly-Up was never once eliminated. Otherwise, that occasion as a youngster in Dublin was the only time in his long and honourable career that he ever refused in front of a fence. Frank never returned him to

Dublin and the little grey horse never looked back, bar the time he nearly died at home.

Frank had bought a new horse, a bay called Westcourt, from Tommy Brennan's father Mattie in Kilkenny, after watching it at Burton Hall. He stabled it in a former cottage that Frank had converted to a double stable, pending his building the new stables at Carrowmore. Dandy was in one side and the new horse in the other. During the night they must have had a fierce fight and in the morning Dandy was found lying motionless on the floor, covered in bites and kicks, unable to get up. In spite of regular veterinary treatment, he lay there for weeks, virtually wasting away.

One day an English vet was visiting, and he suggested it was muscle damage to a shoulder and suggested operating on it. He gave a 50:50 chance of success.

It was like opening a can of worms: buckets of corruption poured out of the incision made and by the time the vet had finished the filthy matter had spread right across the yard. When the little horse came out of the anaesthetic it was as if relief was spread across his face. He got up, walked around, and every day brought improvement.

Only a few short weeks later Frank saddled him and rode him down to the back field. There, he popped him over a few fences, and he was fully sound. Frank brought him back to the stable, clipped him, and told a surprised Cecil Mahon that he was taking him, unshod, to Boyle Show the next day.

There, Cecil won all three of his competitions. It was just as if he'd never been away.

'He was so reliable that people almost turned away when he was jumping knowing what the result was going to be,' Frank says. 'Only once do I remember him having a fence down, and that was at a show in Enniscrone. People said, "He's finished," but I said, "not at all.""

Ballina was another local show, and Frank remembers the high wall jumping continuing until it was nearly dark.

'But the people wouldn't go home. There were thousands of them, it was their interest of the year.'

This was also the time when there was no winter show jumping, and so Dandy was turned out on the farm, along with others, during the off season. He knew it was his holiday, and wouldn't allow himself to be caught, except by Cecil, who usually carried Dandy's favourite sweets in his pocket.

'I had him turned out on my land in Strandhill, and if I tried to catch him he would take off over it. But Cecil would talk to him, and say "you are coming in" and he did. He talked to him in the stable, too.'

When it came to show day Cecil would call to Dandy that it was time to go and, unaided, he would walk out of his unlatched stable and walk up the ramp into the horsebox, and would put himself into whatever stall Cecil told him to.

At Ballinasloe on the last day of the season in 1966, when Go-Sly-Up had been jumping for eleven years and was still at the top, a man stood beside Frank at the ringside without knowing he was the horse's owner. There was a particularly high fence for the puissance, standing well over six feet high.

'Will the little grey horse ever jump that big fence?' he mused.

'If he jumps that he'll never jump another,' Frank said.

The man, not knowing the horse, replied, 'You're right, if he jumps that, that'll finish him,' meaning he would be overfaced.

Without telling anyone in advance, least of all his rider, Frank had decided to bring the curtain down on the horse's career while he was still at the height of his prowess.

Dandy, of course, cleared the fence in question, won the class – his 513th – and retired. He had more than earned it. Throughout his career Frank had turned down many offers, including blank cheques, for Dandy. Instead, he kept him as

Go-Sly-Up's last competitive fence – a stone wall which stood six feet, six inches high – and his 513th win

his 'shop window'. There could have been no better advertisement for his wares.

Later that year Frank, Francie and Go-Sly-Up were honoured by the people of Sligo, paraded through the town and given a presentation.

Cecil Mahon, who now lives in Jonesborough, Northern Ireland, grew up in Sligo next door to Andy Dodd's yard and from an early age was drawn to Frank's horses that were stabled there. At first he would be with a group of other little boys, and the lot of them would find the hosepipe turned on them to send them packing. But as a kid Cecil looked and learned how to feed and groom and muck out a stable. He would be taken to a show in the back of a lorry and Frank began teaching him to ride.

'The first horse I rode ran away with me through the town.' In later years he was the proud recipient of the 'green jacket', meaning that he jumped internationally for Ireland.

By the time Cecil was 12 or 13 he began working for Frank and moved with him to Carrowmore when Frank bought the land there.

'He was a fantastic groom with a great affection for horses. He really loved old Go-Sly-Up. You could depend on him 100 per cent. He'd be there day in, day out, and he would drive and would have everything correct at the show for Francie to ride. They were a great team.'

Cecil says, 'They were great times, meeting all the people at the shows. Frank knew everyone and I was never left out, no matter who he was with.'

Francie Kerins had a couple of good 13.2 hand high ponies and used to travel round the summer shows with his brother. He started working for Frank in the mid-1950s, firstly when he was at Summerhill College and rode in the summer holidays,

Francie on Go-Sly-Up

and then he joined Frank full time when he left school. He stayed with him until just before the riding school was opened, when he felt it was 'now or never' if ever he was to go it alone, and he left to branch out on his own in Collooney. He says that during his time with Frank, and especially on the foreign tours, he made many lifelong friends. He married in 1974 after which he reduced his international appearances and concentrated instead on bringing on young horses. Among his future clients was Ann Smurfit. His son, Darragh, jumped on the winning Aga Khan team in 2012.

He was quick to praise Frank for the help he had given him. 'I am grateful for everything he has done for me.'

For Frank, Francie leaving was a shock, especially as he was on the verge of opening the riding school.

'He told me that if he stayed on when the school was built he'd probably never leave and not know what it would be like to be on his own.'

The *Farming Independent* noted that Frank and Francie had for many years been the leading combination in national competitions and 'by their efforts did much to foster what was a dying sport in the West of Ireland'.

After Francie left, Frank was joined by Jim Cawley who was soon much more than a groom. He became Frank's right-hand man and managed the establishment at times when Frank was away. Frank also taught him to ride.

Jim Cawley, left, Frank's groom and right-hand man, with Carn Rowe

Jim drove Frank in his Mercedes, and he drove the lorry full of horses on trips abroad to the USA, Germany, Italy and Great Britain when Declan was riding in juniors.

His first trip was to Germany in 1974 to take over the five horses bought by Peter Eckert in Wiesbaden. Germany was to feature large in Jim's life. He met and married a German girl who came on holiday to the riding school and settled with her firstly in Hanover and then in Frankfurt.

'Frank was a very popular and intelligent man, and a brilliant judge of a horse,' he says.

There was a time when a German author by the name of Ursula knocked on Frank's door and asked if she could see Go-Sly-Up. She was writing a book and wanted to include him. She then asked if she could sit up on him, and couldn't believe her luck when she was allowed to.

'She wouldn't have got near such a famous horse in Germany,' says Frank, 'let alone be able to ride it.'

Ursula rode him down the road, then said she would like to take a picture of him jumping. At that moment Cecil Mahon was cycling along the road, wearing shoes and trousers, so he got up on Dandy and jumped a wall on him.

'The girl couldn't believe her eyes,' says Frank, 'she thought I'd just got a passer-by to jump him.'

Go-Sly-Up – Dandy – lived contentedly on the farm for ten years after his retirement, lapping up attention from admiring visitors.

Frank went out to him as usual one cold and frosty winter's morning, and found him lying on the ground, unable to get up because of arthritis. The horse lifted his head as Frank approached him. Frank knew what he had to do.

Ursula (top) on Go-Sly-Up and
Cecil Mahon (bottom) jumping over a wall

'He was a darling horse,' he says, his eyes filling with tears at the memory of him almost fifty years later.

Go-Sly-Up

With a stately walk and his head held high
And the clatter of hooves on the Irish sod
With ears alert and a flashing eye
This little wonder was a gift from God.

87

So sound of limb and brave of heart
No fence it ever seemed too high;
In his modest youth he had drawn a cart
Now his stardom reached towards the sky.

His name was known both far and near
About him many stories told,
His numerous wins we now revere
As the Anthems play and the flags unfold.

All four came from the Sligo side,
Horse, rider, owner and groom,
And Go-Sly-Up is held with pride
At Carrowmore in Frank's trophy room.

This little champ had so many wins,
Five hundred and thirteen the records show
And fences jumped, we ne'er could count
As we kept on chanting Up Sligo.

You can hear the cheers as he clears the wall
At six foot six or more
And Francie's smile as he seized the cup
Midst the clapping and the roar.

The numerous cups which adorn the shelves
At the home in Carrowmore
And his pictures, too, his story tells
Of his glory jumping days of yore.

Many greats have come and gone
His record try to take,
But his indelible one lives on
May take centuries to break.

10

Thirty-Two County Show Jumping

In the early 1950s the Irish show jumping team came from the Army, including for international competitions. Civilians were not invited to represent their country, end of story. Frank McGarry set about changing that. He also wanted to see a uniform set of rules, and a united 32-county sport, and in time he achieved that as well.

In this pre-television era shows were a great local attraction at weekends. It was a big day out for city dwellers and farmers alike. If the Army could be persuaded to send competitors the crowds were certain to flock in.

Show jumping had been a discipline for the army, especially the cavalry, right across Europe up to World War II, by which time horses were no longer needed in war. By 1949 only Ireland still insisted on military teams for their Nations Cup. In the pre-war years the Irish Army team of Captain John Lewis, Cdt Jed O'Dwyer and Captain Dan Corry had a stunning show jumping record, winning 23 Nations Cup between 1928 and 1939.

The Brief History of the Army Equitation School states:

The brave decision to form an Army Show Jumping team back in the infant days of the State in 1926 has been variously termed an ambitious undertaking, a foray into unknown territory, a mission impossible. But perhaps the best comment on this far reaching development came, at the time from the French equestrian writer, Captain Montergon, when he declared, 'How fine the courage of the young Irish Army thus flinging itself boldly into the water in order to learn how to swim!'

Some eight years later this same author had changed his opinion. Writing in Revue de Cavalerie, he declared that 'Ireland has indeed begun to swim and its swimming master Col Paul Rodzianko chose the proper method'. The master referred to there was the Russian riding instructor, Col Paul Rodzianko, whose genius helped bring the new Irish team from the status of novice to one of the most feared squads in the world.

The formation of the Army Equitation School had come about very quickly in 1926 following contact between Judge Wylie of the RDS, Col Hogan (Quartermaster General), and the then head of the new Free State, President William T. Cosgrave. Through a miracle of far sighted initiative, the funding was found to have Ireland field teams for international show jumping competitions. Its purpose was to advertise the new State and to promote the Irish horse, which in the long run would rebound to the benefit of farmer breeders around the country.

Recruitment began in early 1926. One of the first to be called, Ged O'Dwyer of Limerick, later declared, 'we were all hunting and racing men and knew nothing about show jumping'. Another recruit, Dan Corry of

*Galway, noted 'when we got to the barracks, the only
horses there were pulling carts in the yard'.*

As Judith Draper says in *Show Jumping: Records, Facts
and Champions,* Nations Cups were very much the preserve of
cavalry officers until the mechanisation of the armies forced a
change in the rules.

There were very few rules and regulations in Irish show
jumping of the early 1950s, and there were no timed jump-
offs (in which the fastest second round with the fewest faults is
declared the winner, from those who achieved an initial clear
round). With no timed jump-off, classes would go on for perhaps as many as six rounds until one horse alone cleared the
course that had been heightened for each round. Banks and
natural stone walls were normal features in Irish competitions.

At what was to become the All England jumping course
at Hickstead, in Sussex, its innovator Douglas Bunn introduced its notorious Derby bank in 1961, but southern Ireland
had been competing over hunting type banks for years. Bunn
also included a number of permanent fences such as the Dev-
il's Dyke, named after a nearby feature, a 100-metre deep V-
shaped valley on the Southdowns.

Frank met Douglas Bunn in Hamburg and then won the
opening three competitions on the first three days of the in-
augural Hickstead, all of them with Errigal ridden by Brian
McNicholl. They were on their way back from competing in
Aachen.

Brian McNicholl, whose father had bought The Brat off
Frank for Brian to ride, says, 'Frank always gave his riders the
prize money, and I was able to buy a farm on my winnings.'

When he had visited his bank manager to ask for a loan he
also paid in some of his cheques for prize money. Surprised by
the amount which, on query, the manager learned was from

Brian McNicholl on Errigal in Aachen

just three weeks of show jumping, he immediately agreed to back him for the farm in Limavady, County Derry where Brian still lives.

Frank says Douglas Bunn always went out of the way to help. For instance, if Frank wanted to change a class for a horse, the charismatic Douglas would say, 'You are here to jump, and I am here to facilitate.'

Douglas Bunn understood riders' needs having been a show jumper himself, first on ponies and then on Beethoven on whom he won the Foxhunter Championship at the Horse of the Year Show as a four year old in 1962.

He then booked David Broome to ride Beethoven, while he turned his hand to the business side of show jumping. The liver chestnut Irish-bred Beethoven was by a thoroughbred, Roi d'Egypte out of an Irish draught mare called Fanny. He was bought as an unbroken three year old in 1961 by Jack Bamber, a Northern Ireland dealer and a long-time associate of Frank McGarry's, and sold on to Douglas Bunn.

With David Broome in the saddle Beethoven won the World Championships in La Baule in 1970, the Derby Trial and the Embassy Grand Prix at Hickstead, a speed class in Dublin, the Toronto Grand Prix in 1965, and was in the British team for the Twelve Nations Cups. Today Hickstead hosts the BHS's Royal International Horse Show, the Hickstead Derby, the British Nations Cup, and the Schools Show Jumping championships, which has an atmosphere all its own, and usually has one or two Irish schools competing.

Douglas Bunn continued hunting with the Mid-Surrey Farmers Draghounds for many years, and was responsible for inaugurating the popular sport of team-chasing in England. He was also Chairman and President of the British Show Jumping Association, and was chef d'equipe of many British show jumping teams. He owned another top show jumper, The Maverick, ridden by Alison Dawes.

The main feature and big talking point of the new Hickstead Derby course was the steep ten foot, six inches high Derby Bank. It was designed to provide the ultimate test of horse and rider, but many of the riders disliked it and refused to jump it. Seamus Hayes was an exception who, with his great horse Goodbye, not only negotiated it but won the first Derby competition with a clear round. The runner-up to him was the phenomenal pony Stroller with Marion Coakes (who was to marry National Hunt jockey David Mould). Stroller won it three years later in 1967, and was second in 1968 and third in 1970. He was in three victorious British Nations Cups teams, won an Olympic Silver medal in 1968 in Mexico, and he lived until he was 36 years old. He was bought originally at Ballinasloe Fair and his breeding was unknown, but be is believed to have been by Little Heaven, the same as Errigal and Dundrum.

Seamus Hayes and Goodbye III won the Derby again in 1964. Paul Darragh added to the Irish list of winners in 1975 before Eddie Macken won four times in succession with the famous Boomerang between 1976 and 1979, followed by Comdt. John Ledingham who won it three times – in 1984 with Gabhran and in 1994 and 1995 with Kilbaha. The most recent Irish winner was Waterford's Paul Beecher with Loughnatousa WB in 2012.

Frank McGarry wrote a song entitled 'Hickstead Derby':

I went o'er to London the Derby to see
With Hickstead the venue for each country,
We had Germans, Italians, the French and Brazil,
The Yanks and Belgiums and Dutch us to thrill,
Too-ra-loo too-ra-lay sure we English
Are great and we'll keep it that way.

We got David and Harvey and Caroline as well,
Though Paddy on Forgie you never can tell
With Derrick on Coldstream they'll not let us down,
And with Maclcolm and Graham we're set for the Crown.
Too-ra-loo too-ra-lay sure we English
Are great and we'll keep it that way.

We got Liz and Ted Edgar who sleep in one bed
Well-tuned for the Derby, you bastard said Ted,
With Nick riding Lastic we ne'er got a snag,
By George it's our day, got it wrapped in the bag.
Too-ra-loo too-ra-lay sure we English
Are great and we'll keep it that way

Say who's the wee chappie all dressed in the green?
Oh gosh, he looks smart he's done this for our Queen;
He's Paddy from Ireland, oh he doesn't count,
The silly bostoon's got no bit in his mount.
Too-ra-loo too-ra-lay sure we English
Are great and we keep it that way.

Round after round sure they jumped half the day,
And then it was time for auld Pat have his say,
When the hooter was sounded he went like a champ
And in kangaroo fashion round Eddie did romp.
Too-ra-loo too-ra-lay 'a buachailling go maith'
I was heard loud to say.

When the scores they were counted the clears start again
And the clock went in action to sort out the men,
But Eddie from Ireland scared them of their wits,
For he won by three seconds and that shook the Brits.
Too-ra-loo too-ra-lay I was proud to be Irish
And be there that day.

When he stood on the rostrum the English did cheer
And they hailed this new champ for the fourth time that year,
The Welsh they were clapping, the Scotties all sang,
While girdles of laurels hung round Boomerang.
Too-ra-loo too-ra-lay and that's not the first
Time big wins came our way.

So we toast that wee island that lies o'er the sea,
How you Irish chaps do it is sure news to me;
Then Eddie spoke up, t'was his first time to talk,
"Tis the fags and the money from Carrolls of Dundalk.'
Too-ra-loo too-ra-lay the Paddys are hard
Men to beat so they say.

Irish show jumping courses were more 'natural' in appearance than the brightly coloured poles of England/UK in the 1950s. Slowly, painted fences were appearing at Irish shows, but there were still a number of banks, ditches and stone walls to be found. There were usually just six fences – a bush fence, an upright gate, a triple rail of five sloping poles, with guard (or take-off) rail in front, a single bank (a double and single bank in Dublin), a stone wall and a water jump. There wasn't always water available for the latter, so a cut depression would

be filled with sawdust or lime to make it look like water, be-
yond a low bush fence.

Show jumping was in its infancy in the 1950s in Ireland so
strong competition wasn't a factor, even though Ireland was
the first country to start the sport with a leaping competition
in 1864, but it had progressed much faster on the Continent.
Europe was also way ahead in the field of dressage.

'That's what left us backward, because we weren't riding
well enough on the flat in approaching a fence – the Irish just
depended on jumping, and cantered up to it,' Frank says. 'Then
we started doing a bit more trotting over poles and different
gymnastics, and a little bit of dressage to get our horses more
biddable.'

Another factor was that when they eventually got to the
Continent they found the fences bigger there than they were
used to at home.

The judging process in Ireland was wrought with inconsis-
tencies. For instance, the wall was topped by pebbles, and if
they were knocked off by two front feet the horse was penalised
with four faults, but if some were knocked off by his hind feet
this resulted in two faults.

As Frank says, 'If you hit it with one foot, you could get
one fault or three, so it wasn't a good method of judging and it
wasn't straight forward because it was totally up to the eye of
the judge and not always can you have your eye on every single
pebble. And sometimes a little bit of clay from the hoof might
leave as he'd jump the wall and it might be classified as a stone
from the distance where the judges would be sitting.'

Judith Draper notes, 'Prior to the standardization of rules,
fence judges did not have an easy time, particularly in Ireland.
Horse and Hound of 17 August 1946 has this to say about the
Dublin Show:

In Military competitions 4 faults are counted if the obstacle is knocked with either front or hind legs, except in the case of the wall, where one fault is recorded if up to three stones are dislodged by the hind legs, and two if dislodged by the front legs. There are further penalties if more stones are dislodged. ... Six different mistakes can be penalized over the single bank, including changing leg on the top. There are six for the double bank, too, and in this case the horse is faulted if he does not change!

No wonder Frank wanted to bring across the board uniformity to the rules!

At each show at this time, the showing classes were held in front of two judges in the morning, and then in the afternoon the same two judges would judge the show jumping.

There were no marking sheets. The judge had to calculate and declare the number of faults, and inevitably some mistakes were made. Unsurprisingly, this system produced a good many disputes over which horse had won and, Frank says, 'very often you'd get the wrong prize'.

Frank determined that a show jumping association with a set of rules should be formed. He attended a couple of meetings in Lisburn in 1950–51. There he met Gordon Keating, secretary for the Show Jumping Association in Northern Ireland, and they were adopting the rules of the established British Show Jumping Association. Keating asked Frank to organise an association for Connaught and Munster. Frank persuaded a vet, Dan Johnstone, to represent Munster, and Keating said he would try and get someone else for Leinster.

It was going to be a big job to find all the show jumping owners in virtually half of Ireland, so the first people Frank approached were the various show secretaries, and they invari-

Frank with vet Dan Johnstone

ably coughed up £1 to join the fledgling association. The aim then was to get riders who entered for their shows to join.

The first meeting of what was eventually to become the Show Jumping Association of Ireland took place in 1952 in the Vocational School, Tobercurry, County Sligo (about 20 miles from Frank McGarry's home) with the intention of forming an association along the lines of Northern Ireland and Britain. The secretaries of most Irish shows in the West attended the initial meeting. They listened to those from the North who had a well regulated set of rules already. In the Republic at that time faults in show jumping were given as 1, 2, 3, and 4. By taking on the same rules as Northern Ireland there would be a unilateral three faults for a refusal, four faults for a knock down of a fence, three refusals elimination, eight faults for a fall – which was the world-wide accepted code for many years.

Those from the Republic could see the benefits, and the Connaught Region was established as a result. Harry McGowan was appointed secretary, Frank was chairman and Pappy Connor of Ballina was appointed president. The committee was formed from many different show secretaries: Tommy Kearney from Ballinrobe; Tommy Hughes, Claremorris; Joe Martin, Ballinamore; Harry McGowan, Mohill; Paddy Rowe, also from Ballina along with Pat O'Sullivan, Paddy Coyle from Leitrim, are among those that Frank McGarry remembers. They represented Mayo, Leitrim, Sligo and one or two in Donegal but it was a few years later that Galway came in.

Together, they introduced rules that were as close to the British rules as possible while still being suitable for Ireland; later, the first Irish Rule book was produced. Once the new rules were established in the West, so they were shortly after adopted by Dublin for the Leinster region, and in time Munster was also represented, so an executive was formed with members from each region, representing the 26 counties of Southern Ireland.

Northern Ireland was already well established, and many meetings were held to try and co-ordinate rules, with Frank often travelling to secretary Gordon Keating in Portadown, Antrim, and even as far as Belmullet for meetings, many miles on poor roads.

'It was a big task,' Frank recalls. 'I also drove from pillar to post down to Cork and Kerry to meet people in those areas to try and get them to organise a universal set of rules, and heights and standards, but that was not simple.'

He got on with it as best as he and his colleagues could but eventually they decided the country should be divided into provinces.

'This was a number of years later,' Frank says, 'at first there was just Northern and Southern. It was not an easy job. I know how difficult it must be for the body dealing with the Good Friday Agreement because they weren't very easy to deal with. I kept on attending meetings in the North and kept on trying very hard to get it on a proper footing.'

Eventually, after 'meetings and meetings and discussions', it was decided to have a four-province show jumping association, the Southern (Munster), Connaught, Leinster and Northern Ireland. Leinster was run by B.J. Fitzpatrick, Jim Cassidy, Colonel Jack Lewis and Fanny Peart, Elspeth Daly and Philip O'Connor. Another early member for the Leinster region was Dr Austin Darragh, father of future star Paul. Frank remembers him judging with B.J. Fitzpatrick at charity shows in the Dublin area throughout every summer, and became a firm friend with him.

The next step was going to be more ambitious.

11

Raising the Flag and Choosing the Anthem

Among the top Irish riders of the time for the Army were Colonel Dan Corry with Ballycotton, Captain Kevin Barry with Ballyneety, Captain Brendan Cullinan with Glanmire, Lieutenant P.J. Kiernan with Glenamaddy, Captain Kevin Barry with Hollyford and Captain Ian Dudgeon with Go Lightly.

A later top army rider was Larry Kiely who represented Ireland in individual show jumping at the 1968 Mexico Olympics. He was also a renowned centre forward for Tipperary in senior hurling.

The Army horses were kept and trained at the McKee Barracks in Dublin. Their usual route to the top was that they were bought as 'green' four-year-olds and taken hunting for a year before their serious schooling began. There could be up to 70 horses in the barracks at any given time, some of them thoroughbreds but the majority three-quarter bred quality Irish hunters. The Irish Army show jumping team competed internationally including in New York, Washington and Toronto with success and became the envy of the rest of the world. But at home there were many up and coming civilian riders who were not afforded international opportunities. No civilian men

Mary Rose Robinson on Westcourt

and just one lady rider was allowed to represent Ireland once a year, in the Queen Elizabeth ladies cup at White City, presumably because the army at that time had no females.

Frank's Westcourt came within one-hundredth of a second of winning this coveted cup, ridden by Mary Rose Robinson (later married to Seamus Hayes) in 1961.

'He was like a stag, he was a little smasher,' Frank remembers. 'He was only 14.3 hands high but a thoroughbred by Browning. I bought him off Tommy Brennan's father when Tommy was 16. He jumped higher than Stroller and I cried when he was sold to Pierod'Inzeo.'

Frank McGarry approached Judge Wylie, who was on the executive committee of the RDS and of the Equestrian Federation of Ireland, and pointed out that his horses were winning many competitions at home. It was reasonable, indeed expeditious, that civilians should be allowed to represent their country. He also propounded his wish to include the North; it would strengthen Irish show jumping.

There were a number of riders from the North who were good enough to jump internationally, but the UK had the strength in depth to produce three teams if it wished, while Ireland struggled to raise one, even though Irish riders gained extra experience by regularly jumping on the British circuit. The talented riders in the North then and in later years included Jessica Chesney (Kurten), James Kernan, Harry Marshall, Dermot Lennon, Billy McCully, Brian Henry and John Brooke.

Frank McGarry set about achieving his wish, which in principle was simple: let the whole of the island of Ireland, all 32 counties, be represented in one. Initial negotiations took six years. There were advantages for both North and South. The South could avail of the talent in the North, and the North, being a part of the United Kingdom, was up against riders from Scotland, Wales and England for selection. The UK could produce three teams on the mainland without even looking at Northern Ireland, while the Republic of Ireland struggled to produce one. If those from the North rode for one Ireland they would have more chance of being selected.

Frank recalls his initial meeting putting forward his idea to the North. 'I was lucky they didn't eat me. But I was giving them something.'

Frank McGarry and the young Show Jumping Association of Ireland now set about in earnest to amalgamate North Ireland and the Republic for international competitions. Apart from uniting the two, there was also the matter of allowing civilian riders to represent their country, and of agreeing a selection process.

Frank was adamant that there should only be a 32-county sport for show jumping. He found backing from Judge John

Wyley. In 1956 the amalgamation was agreed to but there followed another two years of seemingly endless meetings to iron out the problems of the flag.

Frank says, 'This was a big problem for the North as they wouldn't jump under the tri-colour and of course we couldn't have national representation without it.'

In the green, white and orange vertical flag of the tricolour, the green represents the nationalism of a united island of Ireland, the orange reflects the majority tradition in the North who were originally 'planted' from Britain and whose King William of Orange beat the deposed King James II at the Battle of the Boyne in 1690, while the white of peace rests between them, a laudable and, one would have hoped appropriate premise.

At last, in 1958, a compromise was reached: it was agreed to use a four province flag, consisting of emblems that stood for each province, and matching saddle cloths.

An all-Ireland team to jump abroad now appeared ready to go – but the problems were not over. At yet another meeting between North and South, in a restaurant in Lisburn, a man called Dr McNab stood up and asked, 'If you're going to jump for your country what national anthem are you going to play if you win?'

Frank said there was only one, but the man persisted: 'No, no Northern person would stand under the tri-colour or listen to the Soldier's Song being played.'

In a blow, Frank recalls, 'that ended all our years of discussions and we had to start all over again.'

This took another two years of sometimes tortuous debates. Finally, the four province flag and saddle cloths were again agreed upon for international competitions, with the exception of Nations Cups, for which the tri-colour flag and saddle cloths would be used.

Next for the anthem.

It was the issue of the national anthem that brought more problems than the flag when Frank was bringing the North and South of Ireland together as one unit for show jumping.

Frank was chatting one day with an elderly lady called Lady Dorothy Mac, a great follower and patron of show jumping, when he was summoned to an urgent meeting in Dublin.

'That'll be either the flags or the anthem,' Lady Mac mused.

Frank saw her again after the meeting and she asked if they had found an anthem for the Show Jumping Association.

'Yes!' then, tongue in cheek, Frank called out, 'Did Your Mother Come from Ireland?'

In fact, the anthem chosen was 'St Patrick's Day Parade', and for Nations Cups, the 'Soldier's Song'.

One civilian team of Leslie Fitzpatrick, Tommy Brennan, Tommy Wade and John Brooke with Omar Van Lanegan as chef d'equipe had already been invited abroad a year or two earlier, but before the green jackets were universally used.

John Brooke was son of Northern Ireland's third Prime Minister, Sir Basil Brooke, 1st Viscount Brookborough. John faced a dilemma about jumping under the tri-colour. It would mean, if the team won, standing to attention under the flag to the national anthem of another country to that of which his father was premier. It was a problem he discussed with Frank when out hunting with him. He decided to go and took two good horses, Tirenny and Dun Forest. However, in due course John Brooke changed his mind and did not go on a team again. Subsequently, he retired completely from international competition.

When they jumped as a team the Army looked smart in their uniforms; most Irish civilian riders wore black, red or even grey jackets.

'We decided we should be smart too when we were going out as civilians to jump for Ireland, so we agreed on the green, hence the green coats that are worn today,' Frank says. At first it was considered they would be too expensive, but Frank found a willing sponsor for them in Joe McGrath, although in the event this was not needed as all the riders bought their own.

Now, at last, there really was an all-Ireland civilian team complete with uniform and logos, and in August 1962 they travelled to Ostend and Rotterdam.

12

Early Internationals,
Ostend and Rotterdam

Frank was chef d'equipe and took with him all the necessary flags and saddle cloths. In addition, realising that a foreign band was unlikely to know the tune of 'St Patrick's Day Parade', he took a record of it in case they won.

On the team were Billy McCully and his wife, Claire, who was to jump in the ladies competition; Elsie Morgan from Waterford with a horse called Rooney; Tom Morgan; and Heather Moore. Frank owned two of the team horses, Smokey Joe and Go-Sly-Up, both grey; they were also still young and green.

The chef d'equipe's job can be summarised as looking after the riders, especially those suffering nerves on their first international trip, giving them advice, walking the course with them and in general being their mentor. In addition, he is responsible for making the entries for the various jumping classes, and ensuring the riders warm up and arrive in the collecting ring in time for their class.

The journey over was itself a bit of an adventure. The boat got into trouble en route when a storm brewed (Frank thought, 'oh no, not again,') and the captain had to put to anchor. The boat arrived two days late and the horses on board had only a rope between them. One or two may have had a piece of sacking between the makeshift stalls which were barely wide enough for a horse to lie down in – all a far cry from the luxury horse transport of today.

The storm caused the partition poles to break and before long valuable show jumpers, newly purchased horses from Dublin Horse Show, mares, stallions and geldings, were all mixed up together.

'I had a groom called Patsy McElroy, he was an excellent fella and kept mine safe,' Frank recalls, although on arrival his two white greys looked like a pair of blacks.

Frank hired a small bus as that could take all their gear including saddles, and a couple of the English, David Broome and Fred Welch, came along for the craic. (Fred married Sue Cohen in 1962; he was on 21 Nations Cups teams, and died in 2010.) At last they reached Rotterdam, but then found the hotel they had been booked into by the Federation in Dublin was not expecting them until the next day. They could find nowhere else to stay and drove on to The Hague where again virtually all the accommodation was booked. They were beginning to think they would have to sleep on the side of the road, but eventually they were put up in a small house.

'It was most amazing, very small but the man running the place said he wouldn't see us stuck,' Frank says. 'The girls were put in one room, the men in another, and I had a little pouch bed with a couple of cushions and a curtain round it in the kitchen.'

The following day they returned to their intended hotel in Rotterdam and checked their horses on the showground.

Their opposition was going to be very strong. There was Nelson Pessoa from Brazil, the d'Inzeo brothers, Piero and Raimondo, from Italy, plus good riders from Spain and France, with Eastern Europe also well represented with riders from Romania, Latvia, Hungary, Turkey and Poland. From England there were further household names like David Broome, Fred Welch and Sue Cohen.

But the Irish acquitted themselves well and found it a great experience, until disaster struck before the ladies competition.

It was felt that Elsie Morgan's horse was not good enough, but that Claire McCully had a good chance riding her husband Billy's horse Kilargue, because the opposition was weaker in the ladies, with the exception of Sue Cohen for England, and a couple of French girls and perhaps one from Germany.

Frank lent Smokey Joe to Elsie so that she also would have a ride. She took him out on a routine exercise while Frank popped down to the town. On his return, he discovered Smokey Joe had met a practice pole wrong and had broken his stifle joint.

'He was a little dream of a horse,' Frank says. 'I had all my horses insured for the trip, and he could have been put down but I thought so much of him that I didn't want to.'

At the time Prince Bernard was head of the FEI and he found Frank to tell him he was sorry to hear about the horse. He said there was a good veterinary hospital in Utrecht where he could be x-rayed (which wasn't available in Ireland at the time).

'Prince Bernard's daughter, Princess Beatrix, was very good to me. I had first met the Prince when he was riding in Dublin,' Frank recalls. 'Princess Beatrix [later the Queen] offered to look after the horse for me, she was great. The hospital said they would operate on him and would keep me informed.'

A pioneering nylon stifle joint was inserted, and he recuperated with Princess Beatrix and her sister Princess Irene for nine months at their palace. The two princesses cared for him, groomed and walked him and eventually brought him back to full health and exercise. As promised, Princess Beatrix rang Frank periodically to keep him up to date.

'There was no silver spoon in the mouth about them,' says Frank, 'they were little toppers.'

Princess Beatrix, the eldest of four sisters, became Queen in 1980 on her mother's abdication. She abdicated herself in favour of her eldest son, Willem-Alexander, in 2013.

Eventually, Smokey Joe returned to jump successfully and was sold to Graziano Mancinelli to jump for Italy.

'He was a freak,' Frank says. 'He wasn't big. He was by a Connemara stallion called Calla Rebel, and the dam was a 13.2 hands high pony called Irish Peach.'

Smokey Joe showed promise at four and was nearly 16 hands high. He was going so well that Frank bought the dam, and then went looking for the stallion. It turned out he was the teaser to a thoroughbred stallion stud in Kildare and Smokey Joe was his first foal. He bought him but the first progeny between him and Irish Peach died within an hour; it turned out their blood was incompatible.

Frank then put her in foal to another stallion. She had already produced Smokey Joe's brother, Little Model, who grew to 15.3 hands high for Mrs Brenda Williams. They competed in the 1960 Olympics in Rome, and came third in the unofficial European Championships in Aachen in 1961.

Irish Peach produced a 16.2 hands high horse by Midlander that also went to Mancinelli in Italy, and Sligo Peach, who grew to 16 hands high and was sold to Sweden. She might have been only 13.2 hands high, but Irish Peach had no problem in foaling these progeny.

Apart from the mishap to his Smokey Joe, Frank remembers Rotterdam Show for incessant rain and for the craic.

'It absolutely poured down and the arena became a quagmire. We had to tie up the horses' tails and they all had to be washed every evening. It was sad for the organising committee because it was a really lovely, attractive show.'

They faced many fences that they had never seen before, such as dykes and bridges, jumped from different directions, and they enjoyed a great social time.

'There were parties every night, receptions, dinners and cocktail parties, and we made a lot of friends.'

A friend, Ado Kenny, recalls, 'Frank was a great man at a party. He could sing well, make parodies and tell yarns.'

It was the first taste of international competition for these civilian riders.

Frank says, 'I don't know if the riders in the North were grateful or not, but despite the initial opposition, riders from Billy McCully's time onwards like Trevor Coyle, Jessica Chesney, Connor Swaile, Leonard Cave and Harry Marshall, James Kernan, and World Champion Dermot Lennon would never have got a chance to jump for their country, and we would never have known if they were of international quality if a 32-county sport hadn't been agreed upon. They would still have been dependent on England to select them, and England had a wealth of show jumpers and would not have been looking to Northern Ireland. It created a wonderful opportunity for Northern riders to compete internationally that continues today.'

As in other sports today, such as Rory McIlroy in golf, a sportsman from Northern Ireland could opt whether to play for Northern Ireland or the Republic.

As it happens, after the first visit abroad any Irish win was marked with the tri-colour and Irish national anthem, the 'Soldier's Song'. This was because the record of 'St Patrick's Day Parade' somehow got broken during that first trip. 'I won't say how,' says Frank, 'but it caused a bit of trouble with our Northern friends, so we had to fix that up as best we could.'

The end result was that they continued on with just the tri-colour flag and saddle cloths. There were almost certainly a number of Northern Ireland riders who simply didn't put themselves forward for selection, but basically one could say the issue of the flag was 'an Irish solution to an Irish problem'.

However, on his return from this first trip Frank was called in to the RDS and asked what he had to say about the broken record. The future of civilian Irish teams for the foreseeable future hung on his explanation

Frank recalls, 'I was shaking in my shoes. The team was outside, waiting on the fate of our new civilian team.'

Frank said, 'I didn't break any rule – only the record was broken.'

Judge Wylie took out the Rule Book, opened it at a certain page and agreed that it looked ok, 'But,' he said, 'I have a letter here from Prince Bernard and what he says will decide the future.'

He opened the letter and read it out. 'Dear Friends and Federation, I was so happy with your young smiling chef and would welcome him back any time.'

'We never got questioned about it again,' says Frank.

Frank says, 'Our first team was very humble but we had to get international experience and we couldn't get it at home. The Army wasn't going that well at the time and weren't giving us enough opposition. We were able to beat them, but we weren't allowed to go to England as a team, where we could have got a lot of international experience. We could only go as invited individuals at our own expense. We went to Manchester and Liverpool, as individual invitations for CSI but not allowed in CSIO Nations Cups.'

CSI shows (Concours de Sautd'Obstacles International) are international jumping shows, open to riders from the host nation and any number of foreign countries. CSIO shows (Concours de Sautd'Obstacles International Officiel) are official international jumping shows at which a Nations Cup may be staged, one per country (for Ireland it is Dublin, and in England it is Hickstead).

'That first trip was a wonderful experience,' Frank says.

It was the start of the united, uniformed Irish civilian team jumping internationally that continues, although today Army and civilian riders might appear together for their country in one team, chosen simply on merit.

The Army team, meanwhile, still had poll position, competing at official international shows in America and Canada at places like New York, Harrisburg and Toronto. It was preparing for the Tokyo Olympic Games, and it was left to the civilian team to go to Spain and Portugal. The RDS was keen to get those two countries to compete at the Dublin Show in August, and Frank, as chef d'eqipe, was keen to take them there.

'I had the backing of Judge Wylie who told me to do what I wanted and they would support me.'

13

Spain and Portugal

Frank's second trip as chef d'equipe to a civilian team was to Spain and Portugal in 1964. The trips to the USA and Canada were still the province of the Irish Army team. Frank's team consisted of Diana Conolly-Carew, Heather Moore, Patricia McKee and Francie Kerins.

Firstly, the problem of financing the trip had to be resolved. The Republic of Ireland was not wealthy and while there were some riders whose horses were good enough to jump internationally, their owners or riders could not afford to send them abroad. Secondly, Ireland was always a country that sold its home-bred horses (it was the same with racehorses), and inevitably it was likely to be the best ones that not only changed hands but moved countries, too.

This was long before sponsorship, and there was no money coming from anywhere to fund teams, so to try and raise money a scheme called the International Fund was initiated. A pound was collected from as many people as possible, and the RDS agreed to match it pound for pound. This resulted in a pool of £172 by the time the civilian team was to jump in Spain.

The year was 1964 and, as chef d'equipe, Frank was allowed to take the entire kitty of £172 to pay for the travel and accommodation of eight horses, four riders, their grooms and himself. They nearly did not get there because the horses were shunted into a railway siding and lost for three days.

Diana Conolly-Carew remembers the fun that went hand in hand with show jumping. 'Frank had a great sense of humour. The trip to Spain and Portugal in 1964 was the best fun I ever had. Four of us were selected at Dublin show from six applicants. The horses went out by train and we flew but when we got there the horses never appeared. They were lost for three days having been shunted into a siding. Luckily we had brought our own hay and their grooms were with them.'

This was hardly an ideal preparation for an international show. Frank went off looking for them, and before long he was missing too. Eventually, they were located at about midnight and Diana rode Errigal down the street. Her groom, Tommy Tynan, told how Errigal used to snore while sleeping with his nose on Tommy's shoulder. The next day he was one of twenty clear in a class of 120.

Francie Kerins, Diana Conolly-Carew, Heather Moore
and Patricia McKee, Madrid, 1964

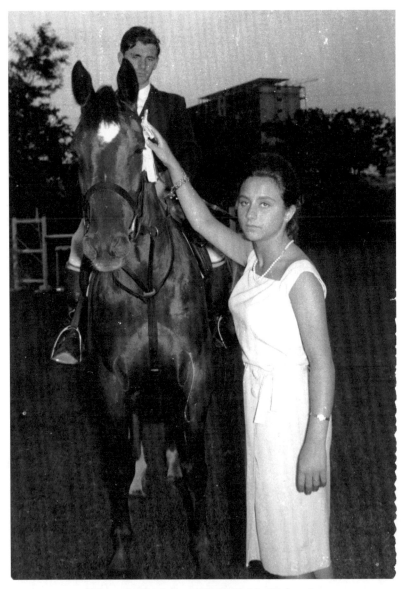

Francie Kerins on Little Toi in Valencia
with a member of the Spanish royal family

General Franco was ruling Spain at this time, and he took a hands-on role as host to the visiting riders. He housed their horses in his stables in Barcelona for the show there and entertained the riders and chef.

In the mornings Frank would arrive at the show wearing a suit but once he had walked through to the chef d'equipe's box he would change into shirt and shorts and give his suit to the driver of his state car, which was provided along with an interpreter.

One day Frank was called to meet General Franco, but he didn't have his suit. He hailed a Spanish rider, Carlos Figueroa, and asked for his suit, explaining why. They swapped in the Gents.

'He was bigger than me,' Frank recalls. 'Someone asked if Carlos had met Franco and he said, "no, but my suit did".'

Frank found trying to make phone calls nearly impossible, and Brian McSweeney of the *Irish Independent* had asked him to ring every day, reversing the charges, so that a piece could be put in the next day's paper.

'I could be seven hours waiting for a line. My sister-in-law was honeymooning about 70 miles away and I went there one day with Diana Conolly-Carew. When I got back to the hotel they told me my call was coming through.'

At a meal with Franco, Frank told him he though his phone service was a disgrace. Franco replied, 'I have got peace between myself and Portugal and I am not disturbing that.'

The pair discussed the economy and Franco told Frank 'the Canaries are my pension for the nation'. This was well before the Canaries became a tourist destination and, says Frank, it was Franco who started the whole development. When Frank first came to the Canary Islands over 50 years ago, there were few roads and he had to go by boat to reach Puerto Rico. The only entertainment was in a canvas-roofed shack called El Greco.

'I was on holiday in Las Palmas and thinking of buying a bungalow but it was all wilderness and I thought I'd be mad to buy.' Today, Frank spends much of each winter in a five star hotel in Puerto Rico.

When Franco put on the show in Barcelona he was celebrating 25 years of peace between Spain and Portugal. The countries were only allowed one team per competition.

'But we had the first green coats ever seen and we got permission to field two teams,' says Frank. 'It was the first televised show jumping and there were 60 million viewers because Franco put on an entire TV network for it.'

Diana remembers, 'One day when we were exercising a military-looking man with a moustache and Labrador came along; he came from Straffan, County Kildare. We went swimming in the sea and he lost his front teeth. Frank took him to a dentist and from then on he had Spanish teeth.'

Another time the Catholic members of the Irish contingent decided to go to Fatima, Portugal, a place of pilgrimage since 1917 when three shepherd children reported they had seen an angel on the thirteenth day of six consecutive months.

'If you see her I'll convert to Catholicism,' said Diana, a member of the Church of Ireland.

On another occasion they decided to go to a bullfight after a fairly alcoholic lunch. The bulls were not killed in Portuguese bullfights but nevertheless Frank, as a cattle man, chose not to go.

One time the team was returning with a lot of champagne, more than their duty free allowance. They poured it into the horses' water containers and then told the customs not to open them or the water would be contaminated.

Another part of that second tour, when they were in Portugal, Frank got locked in the toilet. He couldn't get out, didn't speak the language and still had to enter the teams. Eventually someone realised and broke the lock to get him out.

Little Toi in Barcelona

'We were jumping on the Benfica football pitch when the committee discovered they were short of one international judge because one was unable to get there, and they came and asked me,' Frank says. 'I said I didn't have a licence. But I had been a part of making the rules so I knew them. The organisers rang Prince Bernard who rang the FEI headquarters in Bern, Switzerland and I was given a licence for the show. So that's how I became an international judge. I had to oversee the schooling of my horses and then run to the judge's box.'

The team was away for eight weeks altogether and apart from the originally planned Barcelona and Madrid, they also jumped at Valencia and Lisbon.

Frank was in telephone contact with the chief selector, Colonel J.J. Lewis, and he told Frank the team could continue further around the Continent. What he didn't offer was more money, so Frank spoke to the organisers of the show in Valencia.

'They wanted us there, they wanted the green coats,' Frank recalls. 'I told them I wouldn't even take ten times what they were offering for us to go.'

Most of the European shows in those days took visiting teams and their horses all the way to the national border of the next country they were competing in. They also gave pocket money not only to the riders but also to their grooms. The result of Frank's negotiations was that they were given 'a great amount' and they continued to complete an eight-week tour in total. In Valencia, the team was paraded around the city by the Spanish Army and cannon salutes were fired.

'It was considered the greatest honour to be the chef d'equipe,' Frank told a local paper on his return, 'and the team did not let their country down, and with the wins and places they had in various classes, it must have made an impression on the sales of Irish bloodstock.'

The host country put up the team, grooms and horses, and all Ireland had to pay was the entry fees. Nevertheless, Frank was well out of pocket. On his return he was asked about out of pocket expenses and a donation was made towards them.

Frank was given a civic reception by the Mayor of Sligo, Jim Gannon, in the Mayor's Parlour in Sligo Town Hall, in honour of his two month tour of four shows, Madrid, Valencia, Lisbon and Barcelona. He was congratulated on the team having accumulated 52 prizes, eleven trophies, six firsts, three ladies international overall winners, and first and second in the independent ladies horse competition. It was Jim Gannon, in due course, who suggested Frank use the Sligo prefix in his horses' names. In later years, another Sligo Mayor, James Mc-Goldrick, made him a freeman of the city.

By the mid-1960s Frank had built up a lucrative cattle business. His export business was thriving and bringing plenty of sterling into the country. He was married with the first three of his five children and his life was still a constant round of markets and fairs, working all hours, buying all over Ireland and selling in Scotland and England, with only the occasional night at home. He had also purchased a total of 300 acres of land in Sligo and was earning twenty times the national average. His commitment to show jumping was getting ever more involved. He was not only a leading show jumping owner, with Francie Kerins riding for him, but he was also an Irish team selector. Meanwhile, he had promised his wife Noreen that once he had 300 acres he would build them a house on his land at Carrowmore, outside Sligo.

He was a millionaire, and it was time to settle at home. Frank would still be cattle dealing, of course, but now mostly in Ireland.

Frank with his daughter Sharon on Kilkee King

14

Buying the Island and Building the Riding School

L ife at home was never going to be quiet. When Frank made the decision to quit the export market and concentrate on home, family, farming and show jumping, he was at the time chairman of the Cattle Traders Association, chairman of the Western Livestock Exporters Company, chairman of the Western Show Jumping Association, on the National Executive of the Show Jumping Association of Ireland and he was a selector for the Irish show jumping team.

Show jumping was his first love.

'I decided the best thing was to stop the exporting business totally, even though it was a very lucrative business and therefore hard to give up, but I felt my body was suffering. I was constantly on a train or a plane, or a ship or a car so I had to try and stay at home and be a little more relaxed.'

As if designing and building the country's biggest indoor riding school could count as relaxation!

First he built the promised house, showing what he liked in two houses for his architect to amalgamate into one design. He produced a five, later seven, bedroomed family home, and, after a protracted fight with the local council, roofed it with the

Frank's house with the blue tiles and his latest Merc parked outside

blue tiles that he had admired on the Continent, and were supplied by a London firm.

'They cost more than the rest of the house!' he says.

The house was next to the cattle buildings and stable yard, and he set about building the riding school there, but before that he bought Coney Island.

Frank bought Coney Island, just off the coast of Sligo town, in 1966. Some believe that Coney Island in New York was named after it. Frank was on horseback at the time, and the owner, Michael Ward, was sitting on a wall on the mainland. The two-mile stretch of sand looked ideal for a gallop and Frank asked if he could ride over to the island. There, he found the ground was dry and good and when he returned, Michael Ward was still there.

'That's a lot of land there,' Frank said.

'Two hundred and forty acres,' came the reply.

'Have you ever thought of selling?'

'I'd sell this minute if I got enough money for it.'

There was one road on the island, dividing a pub which was also Ward's home and seven acres from the rest of the land.

'What's your price?' Frank asked.

'Ten thousand pounds and I won't take less.'

It was a lot of money. At the time, £6 would buy a week's worth of groceries. Frank offered him £5,000, and then £6,000, to no avail.

'No, I won't take less, but if you like you can go and look at the cattle and if you like them I will throw them in.'

There were nearly 100 head of cattle on the island and Frank's response was immediate – the deal was done.

Still knowing nothing about the tide between the island and mainland he galloped home, jumped into the car and headed to the bank in Sligo. He withdrew £10,000, drove back to Ward and handed him the cash.

'Will you do me a favour,' Ward asked, 'and take me into Sligo.'

They drove to the same bank and Ward put the money back in. The two men then wet the deal with whiskey in Hardagan's pub nearby.

Later Frank rang his solicitor, Pat Britton, who asked him if he had paid a deposit. When hearing that Frank had paid the full amount he asked if he had the deeds. The answer, of course, was no, so Frank visited Michael Ward who pulled out the deeds from behind a clock on the mantelpiece.

Having sold the island, it would mean Ward having to move but Frank intervened.

'You'll die if you leave, I'm never going to put you out of your house and seven acres.'

As for the luck penny of 100 cattle, they realised about £2,000.

About four or five years later a German investor offered Frank £250,000 for the island; he wanted to turn it into a holiday resort. By the end of the 1970s/early 1980s land prices had dropped by almost half.

After Michael Ward had died, members of his family, nephews who lived in America, tried to claim the island for themselves. Frank said of course they could have it. They could buy it off him, the same as he had bought it from Ward. Frank heard no more from them.

The island had so many sand dunes that Frank didn't have to build sheds; the cattle sheltered in the dunes. It could only be approached at low tide, and then only with care. Frank twice managed to lose a car in the sand, on two consecutive days.

The first was a beloved Sunbeam Rapier sports car. He had 200 cattle on the island and some had wandered onto the strand, there being no fencing on the island. He decided to round them up by car to get them back inland. It was getting dark by that time but all was going well until the car broke down. It wasn't just the car that was stuck, because Frank had three of his small children with him. There was nothing for it but to put one child on his back and one on each arm, and walk through the incoming tide for one and three-quarter miles to the mainland. (Today there are fourteen stone markers that have been driven into the sand at every furlong.)

He got home safely, and returned next day with his groom, Cecil Mahon, intending to rescue the car. Instead, the second car ran out of fuel and it, too, was sunk irreparably by the tide. Cecil recalls them 'running for their lives' to beat the tide. After that, Frank bought a big old Wolseley from Pat Britton and kept it parked permanently by the beach, filled with petrol.

He tells of another time when he bought three farms in one day. He had just sold Errigal to Lady Lauderdale and asked a neighbour called Charlie, from whom he rented land, if he could buy it; the answer was yes. Later in the day another neighbour called Lally, having heard of the deal, told Frank that there was no water on the land. The water came from a lake on his land.

'If you'd told me you wanted to buy some land you could've bought mine,' he said.

So Frank bought that as well.

Meanwhile, as he was waiting for Pat Britton, his solicitor, to arrive, a third man, John, coincidentally called into Frank to say he was giving up farming and would Frank look after his land for him. Frank did better than that – he bought that, too.

When Pat arrived he observed that Frank appeared to be buying land like horses.

In 1968 there was no big arena anywhere in the west of Ireland, and only one small one in Dublin. When Frank wanted to show off horses to potential buyers, he would have to box horses all the way over to the capital.

Among his clientele were the world famous Italian D'Inzeo show jumping brothers, who became the first athletes to compete in eight consecutive Olympic Games, from 1948 to 1976. At Rome, in 1960, Raimondo won the show jumping individual gold medal and Piero the silver in front of their home crowd. Piero won another silver medal and four bronze medals in Olympic Games. He died in 2014 aged 90. Raimondo won two silver and four bronze medals in addition to his gold and died aged 88 in 2013.

So it was logical for Frank to build something for the west of Ireland. At first he wanted to build on the 12-acre sports ground that he bought in the centre of Sligo. Eventually, the football club bought it back with the proviso that for one week a year it would be given over for Sligo Show, but later they fought that clause.

Instead, Frank chose Carrowmore as the site for a complete sports centre, but that was going to be too expensive so he concentrated on an indoor school. He had been across most of Europe with the Irish show jumping team, had seen many designs and especially liked an Italian one.

The arena he built in Carrowmore was a first in Ireland. At 175 feet by 124 feet, it was bigger than Madison Square Gardens in New York. It was surfaced with sand from his Coney Island beach, and he incorporated innovative curved ends instead of corners. 'It can save a horse three to four strides,' he says.

He also built a viewing gallery capable of holding nearly 1,000 spectators, a bar with apartments for students beneath it, an office and board room, changing rooms and showers, and stables for twenty horses. The school would also be used for indoor football and various social events.

He told a local paper, 'I want to bring young riders to the top and develop their talents.'

Although keen to encourage local youngsters, he had also received enquiries from a number of European countries and America.

'I'm no patriot but I have this thing about Sligo and I want to keep it on the show jumping map as much as I can. Of course, it's a business proposition first of all, but if I can boost the area, so much the better.'

Outside, many of the stables today still have their original mahogany doors and stone drinkers (with modern automated bowls placed inside them).

Carrowmore overlooks Sligo Bay in one direction, guarded by Ben Bulben, and looks out on to the Knocknarea Mountains in another aspect. There, Queen Maeve's grave is said to be inside the mound on the top.

'She didn't have a great reputation,' Frank says. 'She supposedly slept with soldiers and then had them put to death the next morning.'

Frank wrote an epitaph:

Beneath these stones
Lies Queen Maeve's bones
But don't you fret or wonder
For these are not the only stones
Queen Maeve's bones lay under.

The riding school took six years and much hard work and planning to come to fruition, at a cost of £59,000, of which approximately one-third came in a grant from the County Development Board.

There was a hiccup early in the building. Huge slabs of concrete had been put down in the ground and steel stanchions erected on them when Frank's engineer paid a visit.

Frank was feeling a bit low at the time because some of his cattle had failed the tuberculosis test, though he was able to isolate them on the island.

The engineer then told Frank that the wind factor was too great, and the building so far would have to be dismantled and a tie inserted in the ground under the floor. It would cost an additional £20,000.

It was a colossal sum and Frank felt pretty low as he was walking down the road, his head full of the building problem so soon after the cattle test failures, when he met a neighbour, John Clarke, with three cows – almost all that he possessed. Frank, who had 300 cattle in his sheds, greeted him.

John Clarke said, 'I expect you are busy – no more than me'self.'

Life can be brought into perspective at such times, and it gave Frank the courage to carry on.

Charles Haughey and former EU Commissioner Ray MacSharry, then a young TD, supported the riding school enthusiastically. It was to have a deep impact on the development and expansion of show jumping and general horse-riding throughout the North West.

On St Patrick's Day, 17 March 1972, Charles Haughey opened the Sligo Equitation Centre. It was an immediate sensation.

It was designed principally for show jumping, with weekly competitions, and Ireland's first ever winter show jumping league. One of its early supporters was Mervyn Clarke, who travelled from Cavan to compete indoors with his horses.

The official opening of the riding school with (l-r) Noreen McGarry, Charles Haughey, Frank Wynne (behind), architect Jim Fairweather, Frank McGarry and Ray MacSharry

He says, 'Frank was the king of the whole horse industry and he ran good shows. He was also an excellent commentator at shows and a good man for his knowledge of horses. He always had time to chat, no matter what. I met a lot of people through Frank. He was also a fantastic story-teller, and very, very good with his poems.'

Mervyn Clarke himself grew up with working horses, but began business life with retail tyre shops and filling stations in Cavan, Naas, Carlow and Dublin. He kept a few show jumpers and show ponies at livery, and then built a small indoor centre himself in Cavan, and started running shows himself, originally for his own children.

Today, Cavan is renowned not only for its shows, but also for its quality monthly horse sales. Mervyn Clarke and his wife Pauline holiday in the same resort as Frank in Gran Canaria every winter.

In time, another big venue was established in County Cork, the now internationally famous Millstreet, conceived by Noel C. Duggan. Frank was one of its earliest judges.

Frank schooling a young horse at the riding centre

Frank talking to an instructor during a class at the riding school

Noel Duggan says, 'Frank's foresight, vision and knowledge of many facets of life have been quite extraordinary by any standard.

'He established the first Indoor Arena in Ireland, long before others had the vision to do so. He blazed the equestrian trial for all other pretenders through breeding, producing and marketing the Irish horse throughout the world. He was a super hunting man for many years and was respected internationally as a highly professional judge of the horse. Frank McGarry answered the call to officiate/judge at Millstreet International Horse Show over 40 years. Frank was the life and soul at every after show party, entertaining all present with his vast repertoire of stories and yarns. A testament to Frank "the gentleman" is after every show at Millstreet, a letter from him always arrived enclosing all meal and expenses tickets he had received and not used! Typical of the man. Frank, I am happy to call you my friend and there will never be anyone like you. You are a Legend!'

Today Millstreet has no fewer than eight outdoor and three indoor arenas, with stabling for 1,500 visiting horses. Not only does it hold a six-day international show every August following on from the RDS, but it has also hosted events such as the Eurovision Song Contest. Most recently, in 2014, it staged the European Pony Championships.

Carrowmore gradually evolved into more of a riding school, although right from the start Frank would be teaching up to 60 youngsters. Frank was always on the look-out for young talent.

'I had 580 new pupils at the riding school and never saw outstanding talent. There was one little lad that might have, Seamus May, and I told his father, but his father said he wanted him to play football.'

Frank's children Sharon, Declan, Philip, Niall and Grania

His own children were all under ten when the riding school opened but in time they all played a hands-on role: Declan, who eventually took it over; Philip, who tragically was to die from a sudden brain haemorrhage when only 44 years old, ran the bar; Niall, who took an interest in course building and the girls, Grainne and Sharon, also helped in the day-to-day running of the business, as did Frank's wife, Noreen.

Today, the riding school only holds two big shows a year: three days for St Patrick's Day on the anniversary of its opening, and shortly afterwards two days at Easter. It also runs a programme called Key Institute of Ireland, which mainly takes foreign students, complete with approved English language teaching sessions. Local riders are catered for, and either keep their horse there at livery or ride the Carrowmore horses for tuition. Up to 100 horses might be housed on the premises or adjoining farm at any one time.

Now more than 40 years old, the centre is run by Frank's son, Declan, always with an eye to the future. While at the start it was the only such facility in the country with competitors and students coming from all over Ireland, there are now a number in the region, so he has adapted. More and more it has become a home from home for foreign students who not only learn to ride but also improve their English. The summer months of July and August are the centre's busiest –when teachers are off school –so giving English tuition to the foreign riders at Carrowmore is a handy boost to their funds.

Declan himself won a European Silver Medal in 1978 as a junior, and at 18 won the Irish Field junior award (Eddie Macken won the senior). He also won a Golden Saddle award in 1978 and honed his skills away from home as a student of

Seamus Hayes presents a trophy to Frank's
son Declan on Curraghill

The riding school today

Iris Kellett in Dublin. Today Declan does a little bit of show jumping locally during the winter, being too busy for any during the summer.

The centre is worth in the region of €1.5 million a year to the local economy. The 'Key' programme began in 1985, supporter by Sligo LEADER (established by the European Commission in 1991 and designed to aid the development of sustainable rural communities following the reforms of the Common Agricultural Policy). Students to Carrowmore generally come from France, Germany, Italy, Spain and Sweden, and they sleep in the accommodation within the riding school or with host families. They learn English in the morning and ride in the afternoon, which might include lessons in the school or gallops along the beach, and social activities are run in the evenings.

Declan says, 'They are mostly already good riders who want to improve their skills – and their English.'

He also operates Ireland on Horseback from April until October. This is for adult visitors to Sligo who take a week-long horseback tour of the county. They stay at a local hotel and have a packed and varied seven-day itinerary. Local people are not forgotten, and there is a thriving trade through livery and riding lessons. Approximately 200 riders a week use the school from young children to adults.

The St Patrick's Day Show remains the highlight of the centre's show jumping calendar, and the three-day fixture sits firmly in the annual diary of several hundred riders in the west of Ireland. In Frank's day top riders like Eddie Macken, Paul Darragh and Con Power all competed there. In more recent times former students have gone on to become international show jumpers such as Ronan Clarke and Michael Kearns.

One of the changes Declan has made is to replace the original sand arena surface with a dust-free Polytrack one that is used in many all-weather racecourses. He also runs a weekly Night Riders group which offers riding to people with learning disabilities, and is nothing to do with midnight steeplechasing as its name might imply.

Declan has a hundred horses at Carrowmore and continues to try to improve things. 'It's a far cry from the day when my father decided to turn 'Up Sligo' on its head.'

Of course, Frank was also ahead of his time, and one of the innovative things he began were the treks across the mountain and down to the beach, as well as longer treks across to the island at low tide.

Saturday Night at the Club

*It was Saturday night and the movie was bad and we thought
    we'd go for a gill,
So we walked for a mile in a breath-taking style till we got to
    the top of hill,
Then we heard a loud noise which caused us to pause, and we
    stepped right inside to a pub
Good feeling was there in a smoke atmosphere. It was known
    as the riding club.*

*The music was sup, there were two in the group and the drinks
    were flying galore,
And the man from the glen called on Philip for gin and Harry
    was yelling for more
Then I heard someone shout give us two pints of stout, a whis-
    key and two little gins
Was it Hughie, Justin or Larry, or maybe 'twas ould Dessie
    Timbs.*

*From the corner a shout, not twenty, I'm out, then I looked
    'twas a table of cards,
And knock after knock on the door, not a lock but never a word
    from the guards,
It was George that had won, I knew by the fun and John Joe he
    lay down his hand,
Oh gee man alive, if I had the five says Cavanagh that would be
    grand.*

*We'll have one if we can for £1 a man; says Walter it's never too
    late,
Arragh run them around, sure it's only a pound, if he sees us
    sure we'll get the gate.*

Deal them, by damn, says Bernie to Stan; says Olive it's time
  for the tub,
And then you might hear a curse or a cheer at the cards in the
  riding club.
The man on guitar was having a jar and he called on someone
  to sing,
And crowd let a roar at Philip for more as the alcohol started to
  sting;
It seems it was a pal as they shouted for Val and every TD got a
  rub,
And the crowd they went hush as he sang verse for verse that
  Saturday night at the club.

Down the other end was a different trend, and the noise of a
  snooker game,
And Foady dreamed and Kathleen screamed and Joe Hunt he
  called for the same;
It was tense and slow as Crystal Joe put down the very last
  ball,
And the loser shook his hand and he said I think it's my turn to
  call
Philip a few for myself and the crew, and the ladies get them
  some grub,
There is nothing austere about the atmosphere that you'll find
  at the riding club.

And then you might see on some poor fellow's knee a hefty big
  piece of stuff
*And someone swear she had a lovely pair or f**k it, sure I've*
  had enough.
Or a nod from the head of Josie or Ned as they step on the danc-
  ing floor,
And Jim Cawley, too, he's taking a few with his lovers, he has
  got three or four,

Or someone been mauled when the last drinks are called, it's
  then they start roaring for more.

*When the clock it strikes two there are still quite a few, and the
ladies on gin are half tore.*
*There is an equine smell from Paul, you can tell; he's Declan's
right hand sub,*
*Good fun in the air, but what a mixture was there, that Satur-
day night in the club.*

*And then we'd discuss the political scene, how the country was
going to hell,*
*With O'Malley and Garrett and Charlie, and the Pope got a
dressing as well;*
*And what Paisley said of the Robinson case, sure he got a ter-
rible fine,*
*And Kinnock he swore about Maggie that she let him down o're
the mine,*
*And Knock, too, how the jets they got through the heather and
bog and the scrub*
*And Casey the Scut sure he must be half cut, was all discussed
at the club.*

*So stop and think, if you're having a drink, or where you ought
to go,*
*Is it somewhere posh with the accent 'o gosh', or with f**kers
that all of us know.*
*Nowhere can you find a better mankind, the good and the bad
have a jar,*
*The friends that you love from the riding club assemble each
night round that bar,*
*And next morning you'd think that I'll give up the drink, my
conscience and soul for to scrub,*
*But the following night you left it half tight with your friends
from the riding club.*

15

Mr Show Jumping

When Frank was cattle dealing and transporting his stock by train the railway porter would check the number and give out a docket, which Frank then took to the office to pay for them. The porter at Ballymoate was Albert Reynolds, who went on to become a successful businessman and Taoiseach of Ireland.

There was a time at the Dublin Show sometime in the 1960s when Albert Reynolds, by now a wealthy man with an interest in horses, was stuck for a lift home with one of his horses. Word reached Frank who readily had the horse transported home for him.

After a show Frank always took his grooms and anyone else who might be with him out for a meal in a local hotel. One day, after Lanesborough Show, they called into the Longford Arms just after 9.00 p.m. and went to the restaurant. Frank did not notice two men sitting at a table.

He was told he was too late for a meal, even one course, because the kitchen closed at 9.00. They could have sandwiches in the lounge if they wished, and the waitress left them. A few minutes later she came back with the full menu. They could have a meal after all. At the end of it, Frank went to pay, but the bill had already been settled.

'Apparently it had been paid for by Albert Reynolds. He was with his brother in the restaurant and had recognised me.'

Frank bumped into him a month or two later and thanked him. 'I didn't see you that night,' Frank said.

'You didn't have to,' Albert replied. 'I didn't have to see you when I needed a horse brought home from Dublin.'

Albert Reynolds died in August 2014 and was given a State funeral.

One of the people Frank met a few times in Europe was Madame Chandon, of Moet and Chandon champagne. She came to Dublin and one time in about 1963 she decided she wanted to give two cases of champagne to Frank. He asked if she could make one of them white wine, which she did.

Frank was never a huge drinker, and one by one he gave away eleven bottles of the white wine. Finally, a number of years later, he gave the last one to his son, Philip, who was going on honeymoon. On his return he insisted on replacing it – but he then discovered the cost of a single bottle was more than £300!

Tommy Brennan sold Madame Chandon a mare called Abbeyville, and she changed its name to Miss Moet.

Frank's sons Declan, Philip and Niall at Philip's wedding

Frank tried but failed to achieve a joint Army and civilian team just a few years after the start of the civilian one. It was 1966 when due to an outbreak of Swamp Fever in Europe there was a ban on Continental horses entering Britain or Ireland so no overseas teams came to White City to jump in the Nations Cup. A special trophy was presented for a competition with two British teams and two Irish teams (Army and civilian) taking part.

Frank approached the Army team's chef d'equipe Colonel Nealan to suggest that Diana Conolly-Carew, with her great horse Barrymore, and Seamus Hayes, with one of the all-time best show jumpers, Goodbye, should join with the Army team's best two combinations, Colonel Ned Campion, with Leitrim, and Colonel Billy Ringrose, with Loch an Easpaig, to form one formidable team, but, Frank says, he did not agree to it. The competition was won by the British B team.

Frank remembers Seamus Hayes as a model team member and gentleman.

'He was always fantastic, no matter where he went. He was probably the world's greatest rider of all time and on top of that a perfect gentleman, one of the loveliest guys to have on a team because he was always obedient. He'd never go along and say, "I want my horses put in such and such a class," instead he would ask, "What have you got me in, Boss?" Until Eddie Macken came along I don't ever remember another rider out of Ireland that was anything like Seamus Hayes. He could ride any type of horse and still get the same tune out of them. He was an excellent rider and a true horseman, and dedicated. Seamus was successful on any horse he rode. He would get a clear round on a bloody donkey or a Charolais bullock.'

Brian McSweeney, writing in the *Irish Independent*, said he was 'the master in skilful riding. Ireland has never produced a better horseman who by performance and sportsmanship has contributed vastly to the upsurge of show jumping in this country.'

The horse that Seamus Hayes was best remembered for was a liver chestnut called Goodbye. Frank tells how he had hoped to buy him at Goffs Sales opposite the RDS, but unfortunately Goodbye had an appalling veterinary certificate (roughly the equivalent of a car's NCT). It said he had a speck in one eye, and splints and curbs (bony growths) on his front and back legs. Not surprisingly, no one would touch him, including Frank, because he wouldn't be able to sell him on.

He was owned and bred by Lord Harrington of Patrickswell, Limerick, and his early education came in the hunting field from Ned Kinane (uncle of top flat jockey Mick), who worked for Lord Harrington for many years. He also won a show jumping competition in Cork in the hands of one of Ned's brothers, Jim Kinane (both are brothers of Champion Hurdle winning jockey, Tommy Kinane, father of Mick).

Goodbye was about five years old when Frank first saw him, ridden by Lady Jane Harrington in Manchester, then in the Ladies at White City. In the end racing entrepreneur Joe McGrath met Lord Harrington who swapped Goodbye for a Donegal carpet for the foyer in his home, from which point him Seamus Hayes took over and went on to win puissance and grand prix competitions all over the world.

Jimmy Macken met Frank one day at a fair and asked him to look at a pony he was thinking of buying. Frank didn't think the pony was good enough but said, 'I like the look of the lad riding it.'

'That's my son, Eddie,' Jimmy replied. 'He thinks of nothing but horses and won't be a butcher in our business. Can he come to you?'

Frank would have taken the lad there and then but a neighbour of the Mackens, Ann Gormley, persuaded Macken it
would be better for the young man to have a couple of years
tuition as a working pupil with Iris Kellett in Dublin first.

A few years later, Eddie approached Frank at the Athlone
Show looking for a job with him. It was early 1972, and Frank
had recently heard that Francie Kerins was leaving him. They
agreed to meet at the pub after the show along with show chairman J.J. Coffey. Eddie Macken felt Frank had a better stable of
horses, and Frank agreed to take him on. He would receive the
same as his long-time jockey Francie Kerins had, somewhere
between £15-£20 a week, from which he had to keep himself.
Eddie was earning £5 a week, all found. At the spring show in
Dublin, Iris Kellett approached Frank and said, 'I believe you
are taking my rider?'

Rather than falling out, the upshot was that Iris and Frank
went into a show jumping partnership, with a joint pool of four

Barnscourt, RDS, 1969

Oatfield Hills, RDS, 1971

international horses, the start of which was that she bought Frank's Barnscourt in order to keep Eddie. Frank told her he had a better horse, Oatfield Hills. She offered £15,000 and in the end he agreed to her request for a 50:50 deal, with Barnscourt to jump in her name, and Oatfild Hills in his.

Then, as now, top Irish horses were often sold abroad. Frank was offered £60,000 for Oatfield Hills by long-time client Graziana Mancinelli, but Iris declined to sell her share. Both were patriotic and wanted the horse to jump for Ireland. In the end Iris bought Frank's share at the original partnership valuation.

Frank came across Oatfield Hills by chance when he went to see a mare, Miss Renwood, owned by Paddy Connaughton, that he had noted show jumping. He told Frank he had a full brother, and brought Oatfield Hills in from the field. At the time he was quite poor but he had a nice pop. Paddy Connaughton asked £3,000 for the mare and told Frank he would also have to buy a cat as his son was breeding them. Frank countered that the two horses together weren't worth that amount, but in the end he bought them both plus one pound for the cat.

Miss Renwood was sold on to Graziano Mancinelli, a leading show jumper who won the individual Gold medal and team bronze for Italy at the 1972 Olympic Games in Munich riding the Irish-bred Ambassador.

After a good worm dose and plenty of food the thoroughbred Oatfield Hills soon proved his worth and reached Grade A the following year.

Eddie Macken went on to be one of the world's top riders and is remembered in particular for his exceptional partnership with Boomerang, with whom he won four consecutive Hickstead Derbies from 1976-79, perhaps the world's toughest annual show jumping competition with its notorious steep ten feet, six inch Derby bank.

Macken was a member of the Irish team in a golden age that won the Aga Khan Cup three years in a row (1977 to 79). His teammates were Paul Darragh (who sadly died in 2005 aged 51), Capt. Con Power and James Kernan. He also won two individual silver medals at the Show Jumping World Championships in 1974 with Pele, and in 1978 on Boomerang, and won or came second in a record-breaking 32 major Grand Prix or Derby events across Europe and in the USA. Olympic glory eluded him, notably in 1976 when, as a sponsored professional, he was barred. England and Ireland almost certainly stuck more firmly to this stipulation than other countries.

Eddie had a reputation for being temperamental and needing to be handled with kid gloves, which Frank as chef d'equipe was not prepared to indulge.

However, Frank says, 'He would probably be one of the best riders in the world both in flat work and show jumping, and he had a great knowledge of what makes a horse tick. And he was hungry to win.'

The Aga Khan Cup is Ireland's premier jumping competition, the country's leg of the Nations Cup, and is the highlight of the Dublin Show, along with the individual Grand Prix.

The Aga Khan donated the trophy in 1926 in appreciation of all the pleasures he had had at previous horse shows and in gratitude of his Irish tutor, Mr Kenny. The Friday of Horse Show week, having no major attraction, was chosen as the most appropriate day to hold the competition for this trophy and this remains its slot today.

Switzerland was the first winner against five other nations, Belgium, France, Great Britain, Holland and Ireland. The United States recorded their first victory in the Aga Khan Cup in 1948 when they became the first non-European winners. America won in 2014 when, much to the delight of the crowd, a team member was Jessica Springsteen whose father, the singer Bruce Springsteen, was among the spectators.

Feltrim, which Frank sold to Charlie Haughey

*Frank as a judge at the RDS in the traditional
bowler of show officials*

By the very nature of his business, Frank had usually sold
a horse by the time it was of Nations Cup standard. His former
horse, Feltrim, which he sold to Irish premier Charles Haughey for his daughter Eimer (now Mulhern), reached that level,
ridden by Tommy Brennan. However, Frank achieved his am-
bition of owning a horse in the Aga Khan Cup with Oatfield
Hills in the early 1970s, ridden by Eddie Macken.

Frank won many competitions at the Champions of the Year
Show at Malahide on the coast north of Dublin, and he was
also a judge there for which organiser Leslie Fitzpatrick, himself a former international rider and lifelong friend of Frank,
insisted that officials wore bowlers. One year Leslie rang Frank
in a panic. The sewers were blocked, could he help? So Frank,
still in his bowler, got hold of some rods and, wearing his white
coat and bowler hat, lay on the ground on his stomach prod-
ding the offensive drain. At that moment he overheard a visitor
say, 'This is such a smart show and just look, even the sewage
man wears a bowler!'

Frank mostly produced thoroughbreds for jumping, and another that made his name over the years was Sensation, who was sold to Italy and set a new national high jump record of seven feet, four inches there in 1969. Frank bought him from Ruby Walsh Sr. when Ted Walsh, the well-known racing pundit, trainer and father of champion jockey Ruby, was about twelve years old. 'Ted asked me for my autograph,' Frank remembers.

Sensation had been turned down by the Army, Iris Kellett and Seamus Hayes, for whatever reason, and by Sean Daly (who didn't consider him good enough for racing) but Frank bought him for £500 and figured he would be able to add a nought on to that sum when it came time to sell him.

It was November and, as usual with an untried horse, he sent him hunting for a bit first. There was one Stephen's Day hunt when, ridden by Cecil Mahon, he approached two walls divided by a narrow tarmac road.

'I thought he was going to be killed, but he was going so fast I couldn't catch him up,' Frank recalls. 'He did it so well, with

Sensation at White City, 1966

just a bounce on tarmac in between that I realised he was some horse. I sent him home after that!'

Sensation went to the opening show of the season at Banbridge on Easter Monday and won first time out.

'I don't remember him losing a competition,' Frank says.

In the Nations Cup at White City, London in July he jumped two clear rounds, ridden by Francie Kerins. He would be the cornerstone for the home team in the Aga Khan Cup the next month in Dublin.

After his performance in London, Frank met with Enrico Pedroni who wanted to buy the horse for Dr Demilia. Frank sold him for £8,000, a huge sum in 1966, on condition that he could jump in Dublin for the Irish team, and the Italian agreed. In the event, however, it turned out the risk was too big to take, and Frank withdrew him from the Irish long list, much to Francie's disappointment.

In Naples three years later, now ridden by Dr Demilia, he set a new Italian high jump record of two metres, ten centimetres.

Another good horse was Sligo Doctor, sold by Frank in 1981, who went on to make a new puissance height record in Nova Scotia, and also won the Grand Prix. In Ireland he was ridden by Frank's son Declan.

Horses like Errigal, Feltrim, Gaillimh, Dooney Rock, Westcourt, Oatfield Hills, and GiGi all won international fame at home and abroad. Irish Coast, sold in 1969, and Irish Tweed in 1964 were also sold to Italy and both represented the junior team there. Westcourt set the ball rolling in the early 1960s when Frank sold him to Piero D'Inzeo; he won five international competitions with him in Milan in 1969. Irish King was sold to a Swiss buyer in 1969 or 1970. At one time there were five horses produced and sold by Frank who won in five different countries.

In a paper of May 1970, a reporter posed the question:

One might ask from where these horses come. Many are bought in the West of Ireland and are broken in at the Carrowmore stables by Mr Kerins while others have already received elementary schooling. However, the exceptional training they receive seems to be the vital factor for rarely does a McGarry horse fail to live up to expectations. And this is the real secret of Mr McGarry's success – the early education of an inexperienced horse which almost always results in graduation with honours.

Frank also remembers spotting David Broome at Manchester Show in 1958, riding a horse called Wildfire.

'He was such a natural rider and so versatile. He could get up on anything. I tried to get him for me but his father was a dealer and so he wasn't free to come. I remember at the end of the show Lady Mary Rose Williams asking if I'd seen anything I like, meaning horses, and I said yes, David Broome.'

Only two years later, at the age of 20, David Broome won the first of his two Olympic Bronze medals on Sunsalve in Rome. He won his second Olympic bronze medal for Britain in 1968 on Mr Softee. He was World Individual Champion in 1970 on Douglas Bunn's Beethoven and a member of the gold winning World Champion team in 1978. He also won the prestigious King George V Gold Cup in the UK a record six times on six different horses between 1960 and 1991. He mostly rode Irish Sports horses of which Sportsman may have been his favourite, and he remained throughout his career at Mount Ballan Manor, Crick near Chepstow. He became President of the British Showjumping Association in 2013.

Frank recalls a time at Dublin Show when Tommy Brennan was riding a big Grade B horse of his, and therefore a comparative novice, called Slieve Bloom. He achieved one of just three clear rounds in the first round when they realised bystanders were listening to their every word as they waited for the jump off in the pocket (collecting ring). Tommy decided to have a bit of fun, and in a clear voice asked Frank what he wanted him to do.

'Do you want me to win it?'

'No,' said Frank, equally audibly. 'He's too green. On the other hand, you could leave out two strides at the wall. Yes, maybe you'd better go and win it.'

Tommy set off like a scalded cat and won by many seconds.

Immediately, David Broome and his father Fred came to Frank to try and buy him. Frank persuaded them to come and see a smart mare that had won three competitions; she was in the practice arena. The upshot was that the Broomes bought both horses.

Meanwhile, Tommy confessed to Frank that in truth he had had to 'lift Slieve Bloom over three of the fences'.

Another time Frank had bought a yearling for his solicitor friend Pat Britton, but Britton didn't want it. Frank persuaded him to buy it for £110 with the promise that he would buy it back three years later.

When the time came Frank had forgotten all about it but was true to his word and agreed a price of £300, although, in spite of good feeding from Pat he was disappointed at how little the horse, Pleasant Knight, had grown. In time, however, he matured into the 'finest 16.2 thoroughbred, all quality'.

Tommy Brennan rode him in his first show at Castletown and when Frank rang him later to see how he had fared Tommy told him, 'I thought we'd have to shoot him to get him down, he was going that high!'

He won six competitions in a row and was eventually sold to the Army.

In 1974 Frank was at a show in Palermo, Sicily, when he got badly bitten by mosquitoes. It was so serious that he was taken to hospital and put into a two-bed ward where there was another patient suffering from the same trouble. The two men chatted, of course, and Frank noticed what a fine voice the other had.

'He had a beautiful accent and was very straight forward.'

Later, after he had been discharged, Frank learnt that his fellow patient was Richard Burton.

'But he was just another person to me.'

Frank joined the board of Bord na gCapall (the Irish Horse Board) in about 1972 when Liam Cosgrove was Taoiseach, and had two five-year stints which included being chairman of the marketing division, by the end of which Charles Haughey was Taoiseach. The board folded in 1981.

During his stint on the board, in 1978 when the market was very depressed, a mixed bag of seven horses, ponies, stallions and Irish Draft show jumpers were taken out to Essen, Germany as an example of the sort of stock available to buy in Ireland. It included the Irish Draft stallion Flagmount Boy, and a Connemara pony Ashfield Bobby Sparrow who went on to become Junior European Show Jumping champion. There was one particularly nice horse owned by Mrs Patricia Nicholson of Kells, County Meath.

Frank remembers, 'We had numerous customers for him, but we couldn't sell him because we had agreed with the Irish Horse Board that the ones we took over were not for sale! All we could do was say we have more horses like these at home.'

While in Essen Frank passed a stand where a woman had a sewing machine, and beside her was a video showing a film of where her materials came from. The board was spending large sums of money sending horses abroad, but seeing this stand gave Frank food for thought, and as a result he introduced video sales of horses at several European venues.

One was in Verona for which twenty horses had been filmed walking and trotting in hand, loose schooled over a pole and then, if the horse was already broken, it was ridden on the flat and over fences. Seventeen of the twenty horses were sold.

In 1979 Frank suffered a run of bad luck that no one hopes to experience. Losing any horse is tough but that summer Frank lost three horses in three weeks, none of them when being ridden.

At Hickstead that July Frank's horse Nephin Mor won three competitions, including in the main arena for his up and coming son, Declan. Little could he have guessed what a disastrous spell was to follow. Frank was lunging Nephin Mor in the Carrowmore arena the day before he was due to travel to Gijon, Spain, for Declan to ride in the Junior European Championships. Hopes were high, and many considered him the favourite.

Frank's right-hand man Jim Cawley was in town filling up the lorry tank with diesel prior to the journey. When he got back he discovered Nephin Mor lying dead in the middle of the arena. He then found Frank sitting in his house in shock.

Frank says, 'I had left instructions not to ride him that day, I would lunge him later. When I started lunging him he was in the form of his life, turning himself inside out, leaping about, he was so full of himself. He was squealing and bucking, and then he reared too high and turned over, landing on his head.

'You won't be doing that too often, I said to him – and then suddenly I realised he was lying there stock still.'

The favourite for the European Junior Championships was stone dead. The horse had broken its neck and died instantly.

When he returned with the lorry, now fuelled for the planned journey to Spain, and sized up the situation, Jim Cawley went out and dug a big hole on the farm and buried Nephin Mor while Frank was still inside.

Frank could have sold Nephin Mor for a lot of money, but had hung on to him to give Declan, who was 16, the opportunity. He had ridden the horse in the event the previous year at Stannington, England and gained a team silver medal. Thirteen countries were represented, with Great Britain winning on a zero score. Ireland was second on a total of four faults. Besides Declan, the Irish riders were Mandy Lyons, Anne Hatton and Trevor McConnell. Declan and Trevor both achieved double clears, with Mandy clear in the first round and one fence down in the second. The Netherlands took bronze, well back on 16 faults.

The European Championships for Juniors, for riders aged 14-18, are the oldest FEI official championship, having begun in 1952.

Nephin Mor's death was a hammer blow. In a trance, Frank rang the selection committee (of which he was a member), and they told him to take a chestnut horse called Sligo Bells. To his credit, the substitute won a competition, and jumped two clears in the Nations Cup competition for the European Championship and the team finished in joint fourth place, just out of the medals.

Graziano Mancinelli, with whom Frank had dealt in the past, made him a good offer for the horse.

'To be honest, I wanted to sell everything,' Frank recalls. 'I was so down, and I got a good price for him.'

More disappointment followed. Frank had given Nephin Mor's full sister, Sligo Fox, to Jimmy Maguire to jump and sell in England. When Jimmy rang to say he had bad news, Frank thought he meant he hadn't succeeded in selling her. Instead, having taken her to a show, something caused her to suffer a brain haemorrhage and she bled to death.

Within three weeks of these two tragedies, a mare was brought in from grass. On her first night in something caused her to hit her head on her feed manger and she was found dead in the stable next morning.

A few years earlier, in the mid-1970s, Declan's top pony Curraghill was stolen at Ballinasloe Show, which is run in October in conjunction with the world-renowned Ballinasloe Horse Fair. He had jumped in his class, and was then loaded back on to the lorry while the horses were taken off to compete in their classes, a process that is followed dozens of times a year amongst competitors.

Frank was sitting in the judge's box when he received a message to say the pony was missing. The police were immediately informed, and the ports alerted. One crucial description Frank was able to give was that the pony, most unusually, held his tail cocked to the right. Curraghill was not the only pony stolen that day, and at length the police rang Frank to say they thought they had found his star in a field full of other stolen horses, but for one thing: the pony in question carried its tail to the left. It was the right pony – it was just that Frank had got the tail posture the wrong way round.

16

Saving Carrowmore

Beside Carrowmore and over the road from it lies Ireland's largest and probably oldest of four megalithic passage tomb complexes, including Newgrange in the Boyne Valley of County Meath. The tombs at Carrowmoreare are around 5,000 years old.

As a result of land clearance and sand and gravel quarrying, particularly in the nineteenth century, some 25 tombs are known to have been destroyed at Carrowmore. Today 30 remain, of varying sizes. Most of the chambers are small polygonal structures that are open at one end and have, or had, a conical stone on the roof. One bears the only known example of tomb art, decorations incised into the front face of the roof stone which can be seen in certain light conditions.

That the site is today one of County Sligo's most sought after visitor attractions is due in no small measure to Frank McGarry and a number of other locals without whose determination it might have become a venue to avoid.

In 1983, Sligo County Council bought a disused sand quarry just over a small lane from one of the monuments and began using it as a landfill dump. At once alarm bells began ringing within the community. Two neighbours called on Frank to discuss the matter, and he was appointed chairman of the subsequently formed organisation against the dump, along with Neil Crimmon, John Hamilton, Paddy O'Hara and Patricia Mulligan who was secretary. Calling themselves the Carrowmore Residents Association, it was the start of a six-year fight.

'The dump was near springs and was likely to pollute the water, as well as being beside megalithic tombs,' says Frank.

He wrote to the county manager and obtained an interim order. The group lobbied county councillors, but were defeated 10-9 in the council vote that followed.

'Eggs would be on our faces if we didn't proceed further,' says Frank. 'The tombs were a tourist attraction with the potential to become a major one.'

The last thing visitors would want to see, they reasoned, was an unsightly and possibly smelly landfill site.

The group called on a hydrologist from Cambridge who he proved that there would be seepage into the springs if the dump went ahead, and they obtained a solicitor who said a

Megalithic tombs at Carrowmore

temporary injunction would be needed to stop the dumping. A strong deputation went to the county manager asking him to stop.

They approached the Tourist Board, An Taisce, Board of Works, and Office of Public Works (which looks after national monuments), but not one of them came onside, in spite of promises of assistance. The residents were left on their own. The group consisted of 17 or 18 local residents plus two MEPs, Ray MacSharry and Joe McCartin. Unfortunately. the parish was split. One local vendor stood to gain a lot of money from the project, and residents were divided.

The County Manager continued to insist that he had a mandate but, Frank muses, should one person be able to destroy an ancient monument? The group approached him again, but his mantra was the same: 'I have a mandate.'

The group now had to decide whether to pull out or to take him to court. They needed to pay legal fees, and households were asked to pay £500 each. More than £10,000 was raised and the solicitors sometimes worked until midnight on the case.

One of them, Pat Britton, cautioned that to win would 'be as unlikely as getting the first horse you ever owned to the Olympic Games.'

Three years later the case finally went to the High Court.

'It was a funny case,' Frank says. The judge gave the county manager a back door by which he could get out, by stipulating certain conditions, including that he must prove there would be no leaking, and then to come back to the judge for a full decision. He awarded the group half their expenses.

When they came back before him, the judge delivered his final verdict. It was 4.45 p.m., just fifteen minutes before he retired from office. It was his last ever case, and it went against them.

So the group called a meeting to decide what to do. It was difficult to persuade them to continue because of the cost. Frank, the bit between his teeth, said he would go on his own, and would go to the European Court if necessary; he was determined to get justice eventually. After tough wrangling (because of the likely cost involved), Frank persuaded the group to appeal to the Supreme Court.

There was to be another three years of hard work by those remaining in the group, and Save Carrowmore car stickers were sported not only locally but also in Belfast and as far away as New York.

At one time, the county manager threatened Frank, saying, 'I will take the blue slates off your house.'

On another occasion Frank heard that the Taoiseach, Garrett FitzGerald was coming to Jury's Hotel in Sligo and Frank decided he wanted to meet him. Frank was used to getting the run-around and asked a TD, Ted Nealon, to assist him, telling him it was a matter of international importance. The Taoiseach was on a new-fangled mobile telephone, talking 'a mile a minute', and was still on the phone when the TD had to leave for Brussels, telling Frank it would not be possible to introduce him. Undaunted, Frank confronted Garret FitzGerald and gave him a piece of his mind. (Ted Nealon died in January 2014.)

On the day of the Supreme Court judgement in 1989, Frank was in Arizona with the Irish show jumping team. The case lasted barely twenty minutes before the Supreme Court judge complimented the group, ruled in its favour, and awarded it costs.

Carrowmore

Through this life we pass just once
Worrying of things that seem so grand
And do not think of those from thence
Passed five thousand years ago this land!
Beneath these hefty rocks are laid
Forefathers of the present Carrowmore,
With furrowed brows and sweated hands,
Have paid a price for us forever more.

The pugilists of society came,
Options seized on this great place,
And powerful people permit sought,
That earth of God to change its face.
Mighty men from high places came,
Peered at peasants from Carrowmore,
Forget did they that better men
Had trod five thousand years before.

A few small beings conditions laid
To bureaucrats of the great state,
To leave alone this secret place,
Or else that we'd decide its fate.
But power and might our quest did crush,
Still strong in mind and heart and will,
But started on this Sacred ground
A rubbish dump they called landfill.

Six years of legal battles passed
And favoured they who sought this wrong,
Undaunted by the powers that be,
Our purse was weak but spirits strong.
Again we rose for the highest court,
Supreme it's called in our land.
Their battle soon it came to grief,
Three wigged men on the bench did stand.

Their delivery it was loud and clear:
All of you to whom concern,
These learned men they spoke as if
Each one of us discern,
This group of people they have set
Example, plus their pride
And courage to preserve this land,
And that's what we decide.

Historic graves they lie beneath
The hill of Knocknarea,
And thousands come to pay respects
To these ancient tombs by day.
Let's not forget the men who fought
That battle to preserve,
The graves of those 'neath Megaliths
And the credit they deserve.

17

The American Dream ...

American film director, screenwriter and actor John Huston loved hunting with the Galway Blazers and kept a home near Craughwell to indulge his passion each winter. He had a particular hunter called Errigal that out of season, when Huston was usually back in America, would be ridden by his secretary Mary Kelly, and show jumped by Paddy Lynch.

'I fancied the horse,' Frank recalls, 'but I knew John Huston wouldn't be on for a sale.'

Baroness Diana Wrangle (née Conolly-Carew) remembers, 'John Huston's third wife wanted him for hunting herself.'

For about two years Frank observed the horse at local shows, and one time saw him win three competitions in a day. He felt his chances of bidding for the horse were low, but eventually he was granted an appointment with the world famous film man in his Galway home. When Frank arrived Huston was wallowing in a steaming sunken bath, a cigar in one hand and a brandy in the other.

'That's the way he was,' Frank says.

At length, Huston asked £1,000 for the horse, which was at a time when £1,000 would buy a nice house, and £200 would buy a good three-year-old hunter – and that was it, no bartering.

Frank retired to wait for him in the antique-furnished drawing room. Huston came in, now dressed, for a drink and a chat.

'He seemed a down to earth sensible guy. I told him I wanted the horse for show jumping and he said he hoped he would be successful.'

Frank asked him for a luck penny but he didn't know what that was, so Frank took out his cheque book and paid him the full amount.

Errigal stood only 15.2 hands high and was by Little Heaven, who was also the dam of one of Ireland's most famous horses, Dundrum, who, little more than a pony, was ridden to huge success by Tommy Wade. He was possibly also the sire of the phenomenal pony Stroller.

In America, however, when preparing for the Irish team competing there, he began breaking blood vessels. Diana Conolly-Carew was taking her great horse Barrymore, but two horses were needed and she had lent her other one, Pepsi, to her brother Patrick (Pepsi had a particular party trick where he used to stand on his hind legs when his rider took his hat off saluting the crowds). As a result, Errigal (who had meanwhile been purchased by the Carews) was sent out to America. They were met by the Irish Ambassador and taken down to Florida, the 'sunshine state'. They were put up by Diana's grandmother, the Countess of Lauderdale, and watched the jumping which was holding the old-fashioned 'touch' jumping, where faults were given if the horse touched the lath on top of the jump. At the time it was permitted to use a bamboo pole in the warm-up area to 'rap' the legs of a horse as it jumped to make it jump higher and clear the laths in the competition. A man did it for $10 a time but declared he would do it 'free for the Irish'. The practice is long since illegal.

Diana and Errigal won the silver individual medal and were part of the bronze medal winning Irish team. The organisers didn't have the Irish national anthem so they played 'You're looking over a four-leaf clover' during the presentation ceremony.

It was in the1980s that the Irish Horse Board realised that 57 per cent of the world's show jumpers at the time were Irish-bred, so they decided to try to interest the American market in buying some. Frank, who was the board's marketing manager at the time, was part of a delegation to New York that included Frank and James Kernan, Harry Marshall, Tommy Brennan and Sean McCaughey.

The best US riders were assembled in the Waldorf Astoria Hotel, including Rodney Jenkins, Michael Matts (one of the nicest riders, say Frank), and Katie Monaghan, as well as Johnny Madden, the trainer of Katie who arranged the venture.

While there, some of the Irish accepted an invitation to hunt in Virginia. Tommy Brennan and Con McElroy both rode while Frank was among those who looked on. The Master was John Warner, a Virginian senator with a 2,700-acre farm in Middleburg, who also happened to be married to Elizabeth Taylor at the time. After hunting that evening Warner invited the Irish guests to dinner at a restaurant called the Red Fox. Among the diners were two sisters, described by Frank as old-timers, and they were all engrossed in talk about hunting. One of their stories that Frank remembers was how their 'lovely yeller terrier' used to run in front of the hounds. Talk was in full flow when Elizabeth Taylor walked in.

Frank naturally stood up, but one of the sisters, Sally Sexton, admonished him, 'she knows nothing about hunting,' and continued discussing the day.

'She [Elizabeth Taylor] was a nice girl,' Frank says, 'though she was getting on a bit – I wouldn't stand in snow to see her.'

So began the American dream that ultimately turned into a nightmare for Frank, but not without some memorable moments along the way, including meeting a number of other world-renowned Hollywood actors.

Following on from this initial delegation, an American contingent travelled to Ireland to check that there were the right sort of horses for them. At the start, they were snowed into their hotel in Stillorgan for three days, and then they viewed eight or nine, and picked out five that they thought might sell.

These were then flown to the USA. They went into quarantine before flying on to Tampa, Florida. When they came to collect the horses out of their quarantine quarters it was discovered one of the horses didn't have its passport because it had been left with shipping agent Eddie Brennan by mistake. When a fax machine was used to sort out the problem Frank could scarcely believe his eyes at such technology. He also was amazed at the sheer size and scale of the United States.

At Disneyworld, Con McIlroy, Tommy Brennan, Frank McGarry and Frank Kiernan

The horses then spent five days jumping at the Tampa Show, followed by an auction sale, but only Tommy Brennan's horse got sold.

So this first visit to America elicited limited success, but there were many more horses at home and Frank realised that it was no good just telling people about them and showing them photographs; they needed to see them in the flesh.

The second US trip was to Griffith Park, outside Los Angeles, where the Irish horses were stabled. Griffith Park is set in 75 acres and houses livery horses as well as staging shows. While riding out there in the mornings, Frank met many stars. One was Dennis Weaver of the TV series 'Gunsmoke', who kept horses there.

During this visit, Frank and Tommy Brennan were not doing as well selling their horses as they would have wished. In

John Kenehan, Con McIlroy, Frank McGarry, 'Big D',
Trish Quirke, whose husband, John on far right, an American
equestrian magazine owner, brought the group over,
John Cowley and Tommy Brennan

fact, they had sold none of the seven they had brought over. They needed to improve on their contacts or networking. It was very warm and Tommy Brennan, sitting on a tack box, was feeling a bit depressed.

'Well, wouldn't it be worse if you were trying to sell umbrellas,' Frank said.

Another TV actress, Lesley Evans of 'M*A*S*H' and other programmes, who they had also met through riding out there, said she might get Sylvester Stallone to buy one and brought him to Griffith Park one morning. The world famous actor wanted a horse for hacking around on his ranch. Frank reckoned one of Tommy Brennan's would suit, and as Tommy was out somewhere Frank negotiated a deal. He had no idea what Tommy hoped to get for him, but Frank asked £15,000 and the two men shook hands.

Tommy returned and asked, 'Anything doing?'

'I sold your big horse.'

'Great,' said Tommy, 'what did you get?'

'Four thousand,' said Frank, straight-faced.

'Great, I'm glad to be rid of him,' said Tommy – who was doubly pleased when Frank told him the true price.

Frank was then invited to Sylvester Stallone's ranch. He knocked on the door of the wrong house at first, where another film star pointed him in the right direction.

Knowing Frank was a cattle man, Stallone showed him his pride and joy, a big Brahma-cross bullock that was grazing on his lawn.

'What are you going to do with that?' Frank asked him.

'Gee mate, can't anyone even have a pet without McGarry wanting to do a deal?'

Part of Sylvester Stallone's Brahma breeding herd

Frank found further help from another film star, whose Christian name he believes was Emily. He met her at Flintridge Show, outside Pasadena, when they were having a drink in the free tented bar at the end of the show.

'Are you the Irish guy?' she asked Frank.

She promised to introduce him to the biggest show jumping trainer/livery proprietor in the area, Jimmy Williams, with whom she kept a horse herself. He had between 80 and 90 horses and she reckoned he could find sales for them.

Frank suggested they have dinner together at 6.00 pm the following evening and Frank, not knowing the area, asked her to book it. The Irish were staying in the Beverly Hills Hotel.

When they heard about it, Tommy Brennan, Kevin Bacon and company teased him, saying some hope he had of picking up a glamorous film star; they doubted she would turn up.

On the dot of 6.00 pm the star arrived in a chauffeur-driven convertible Rolls Royce, along with her bodyguards (as all the stars had). At this, Tommy Brennan and most of the Irish contingent, about nine of them, decided they would come along as well.

'Hang on,' she said, 'it's not that easy, it's kinda exclusive.'

She rang the restaurant, the La Sere, to fix it.

When they arrived, a red velour carpet was laid out under a tunnel awning and they were met by staff carrying open parasols to lead them in. Tommy Brennan whispered into Frank's ear, 'This will cost a gee [thousand] each.' The day before in Los Angeles he had seen two film stars pay $250 each for a lunch that would have cost five shillings in Ireland.

Once inside, Emily ordered a cocktail, so all the Irish followed suit, soon followed by another one. These were followed by pink champagne, and then the menus arrived, each one in a new pigskin leather case for the recipient to keep. Each diner had an individual waiter.

A lavish and memorable five-course meal followed, with plenty of bonhomie and craic. It was gone midnight when the bill – in another pigskin case – was presented to Frank. As he says, it was he who was taking her out. Tommy Brennan was beside him and saw the total: $10,800. Tommy promptly excused himself and went to the toilet, rapidly followed by a number of the others including, Frank believes, himself.

When they were back and re-composed, Tommy jingled a glass and stood up.

'We have here the chairman of Bord na gCapall, and I'm sure he would like to say a few words.'

Frank stood up, extolled the virtues of Irish horses, and finally thanked Emily so much for a wonderful dinner.

To her credit, Emily simply took out her card and paid for the whole evening without demur.

Film stars were not an unusual sight at Californian horse shows. There was a time when Frank had won a class but he noticed people kept coming up to someone else who hadn't won, asking him for his autograph.

'He was a nice little fella, about the size of Charlie Haughey. He invited me for a beer, and we had a couple in a tent. I said to him, "why do people want your autograph – sure, you didn't win anything?" He replied, "Well, it's not about that," and said no more on the matter.'

Outside the tent Tommy Brennan and Con McElroy were sitting on the grass. When Frank joined them they said, 'When you go home, Frank, tell your children you had some beer with Paul Newman.'

Frank was invited to dinner at another bar food restaurant, Budds in Carmel, by Gerry Martin, a surgeon who lent him a bungalow in nearby Pebble Beach. Budds was owned by Woody Allen, a friend of Martin's. Clint Eastwood lived on the other side of the road.

Another restaurant they went to was Lesley Evans' invitation-only Penelope's in Santa Barbara. Tommy Brennan was again among the party and, seeing Frank Sinatra dining at another table, waltzed over to him and said, 'hello, ol' blue eyes,' and then indicating towards Frank McGarry, said, 'I have a singer here, too.'

At the end of the meal, the Irish ordered Irish coffees but when they arrived they were not correctly done so, requesting what he needed, Frank promptly made them the traditional Irish way.

18

... That Turned into
a Nightmare

Frank's next US visit was under his own steam, independent of the Irish Horse Board. He had sold a good pony
for about £20,000 to a man in America, who had been pleased
with a previous purchase from Frank. Frank sent this one over
along with Leapy Lass that he had sold to Molly Martin of Pebble Beach, and Sligo Joker that he would compete with and try
to sell. Robert Splaine won on Sligo Joker in Santa Barbara
and the grey was sold to Rita Shugart, of the computer people.

Meanwhile, the American appeared delighted with the
pony, but two months later he called Frank and said, 'You've
got a pony with me but I can't take him, he's not what I want,'
saying his trainer said it was the wrong height or some such.

Disappointed – for one thing, he knew the pony was as
he had described – Frank arranged to travel down by trailer
for the long journey to Pasadena to collect him. They met at
5.00 pm in the square, whereupon the American said he would
make an offer of $14,000, which would leave Frank with a
large loss from the original deal, but he accepted it. The two
men then went out to dinner and when Frank got up to leave,

the American told him that actually everything was fine with the pony and he was delighted.

'So I've gained,' he said.

'You may have now, but you won't have in the long run; I'll never deal with you again.'

About six months later the American came over to Sligo to buy again. He rang Frank when he was about two miles away and said he was coming to stay with him. Frank told him the house was full and booked him into the Southern Hotel where he bought dinner for him and his wife. The American said he wanted Frank to show him some horses.

'Well, you won't be buying off me,' Frank said. 'The last deal was the last deal.'

Far worse was to come on his next and final US visit in February 1989. He had already taken two horses there the previous autumn, and they were stabled with Jenny Newall. They were Sligo Patch, a grey, and Sligo Special who 'jumped for fun over any height' but who could 'buck you off in a second'.

It began spectacularly, firstly in California, where Sligo Special won the Championship in his class in Los Angeles, and Sligo Patch, a grey, was reserve champion, both ridden as usual by Jenny Newall.

By now a number of Americans were used to Frank transporting his shop window horses by plane to Los Angeles. He was building up a reputation by competing on their soil, something they appreciated as not all of his potential buyers could travel to Ireland to view his horses.

'Jenny Newall was a good, versatile rider,' Frank says, 'and every time she won a competition she would kiss and love the horse.'

Sligo Patch

After Los Angeles they moved on to Arizona for that state's big show.

Frank had sold Sligo GiGi some time before to a Kuwaiti called Hamoud, and the mare had gone on to win a medal in the Asian Games. He met him again, this time in Arizona, and showed him Sligo Special who was due to jump in the Champion of the Desert class in a few days' time. Frank placed a price tag of $250,000 on him. He gave him a leg up, and walked ahead with another Kuwaiti who spoke good English. Next moment he looked round, and Hamoud was lying on the ground with a broken collar bone and his valuable horse was a speck in the distance galloping off into the desert.

Always hard to catch, they could do nothing until, luckily, the horse came back unscathed. The deal, of course, was off.

A couple of days later it was time for the main competition. Sligo Special and Jenny jumped two impeccable clear rounds in the Championship. There was then a break while the course was altered for the final against the clock. There were about sixteen horses left in the competition.

Frank walked the changed course with Jenny and her husband, Steve. There were five strides down to the wall.

'You could cut out two strides there,' Frank said.

'Are you trying to get my wife killed?' Steve asked.

'I won't. This horse is speedy.'

Jenny cantered in and rode the round of her life to clinch the title Champion of the Desert. Sligo Special was now well worth the $1.4 million asking price.

Sligo Patch, meanwhile, was lame, and had been so for most of the trip. He was being treated for a bad back, but in the end it turned out to be caused by a small stone in his hoof.

When Frank met an American-based contractor from Dungannon it was good to chat with a fellow Irishman, and Frank accepted an offer to visit him down at his house in San Diego. It had been a long tour and although Frank had returned briefly to Sligo the two horses had been in California for many months, cared for by Jenny, with neither horse sold. So when the Dungannon man said he would be able to find buyers for them

Frank displaying his Champion of the Desert rug

both, Frank was pleased; another Irishman and a good rider, Damien Gardner could compete on them. Frank was looking forward to getting back to California, and from there to home. He gave the Dungannon man the passports and told him the prices he wanted for the two horses: $50,000 for Sligo Patch and $250,000 for Sligo Special and the two men shook hands.

By March Frank was home, and in April he received a phone call from the Dungannon man to say he had sold Sligo Patch for $70,000. Frank was delighted, and asked him to pay Steve and Jenny their expenses, and the entry fees and any other bills out of the proceeds, and to keep ten per cent for himself.

In about September, Hamoud contacted Frank wanting another horse and Frank found one for him costing £40,000. He went to the bank where a number of cheques had come in but not, he realised, from the man in America, and he called him. He was told that outstanding bills had to be paid and then it would be in his account.

Still the money failed to turn up. The next time Frank rang him he was told he had the wrong code, although Frank had received money from other countries using the same code. When the money had still not arrived in Frank's bank account he called again. The phone was answered by his wife.

'Keep me out of it,' she said. Finally it dawned on Frank that something was up.

Meanwhile, he was blacklisted by the American show jumping body for not paying his entry fees. He also discovered that Jenny and Steve had moved and he had no forwarding address. At length he found a phone number and spoke to them both, but they refused to take any money owed.

In time, it was discovered that the man had transferred the two horses into his own name. There was nothing for it but to try to get them back.

Frank's son Philip was in Boston. He arranged for Jimmy Ritter, who had a show jumping yard, to transport the horse back to New York by trailer, a distance of some 3,000 miles and several time zones. He also rang the Dungannon man to inform him he was coming for him, but was refused permission. It wasn't easy. He not only had the horses but, crucially their passports, which would now identify him as owner. Sligo Patch was sold and gone, and Sligo Special was stabled behind locked gates with Mexican guards and guard dogs. Philip found someone to dart the dogs and got permission from Hap Hanson, a show jumper in the next door yard, to knock down a gap in the wall between the two premises to gain entry. They found the horse all right, but Sligo Special refused to be caught. Philip rang Frank in the middle of the night, and from the description he confirmed it was the right horse, and suggested he elicit the help of Damien Gardner because the horse would know him. Damien came readily, and caught and loaded him. After they were a good fifty miles down the road, Philip rang the man to say he had taken the horse. He said the horse was stolen and he was going to report it, but they heard nothing more.

The saga was not yet over. The horse reached New York but because of quarantine restrictions and difficulties in finding flights he spent the next twelve months stuck there with Jimmy, costing Frank money every day. Eventually, Harry Marshall got him back to Germany and sold him there on Frank's behalf. Frank had lost £110,000 on the two horses and, he says, Sligo Special never shone again.

'But far worse for me was not paying the girls and being blacklisted.'

To a man like Frank a handshake was considered a bond. He never returned to America, and the Champion of the Desert was his last ever international win as an owner or trainer.

He also never rode again.

During that visit in 1989 Frank McGarry, 7,000 miles away from home, spent some of the time staying with Carol Atkinson, Jenny Newall's mother, in the San Francisco bay area. While there, he immediately accepted Carol's request to give a lesson for her in a nearby riding school. One of the clients was Winnie Magowan, a Safeway supermarket heiress who lived in the lap of luxury in an opulent ranch. Her own car was a Rolls Royce convertible, and Frank remembers her dogs being transported behind her in a Lamborghini.

Impressed by the way Frank had given riding lessons to some of her friends, she tried to tempt him to stay by offering him a fabulous house and a number of acres for nothing, subject only to her father-in-law being allowed to stay there also during his lifetime. This was not for Frank, but he again agreed to help some friends for nothing – again – before heading for home. One lady had been so impressed the day before that she asked him to help with her horse.

'They were all spoilt,' says Frank, meaning the horses, but doubtless the same could have been said for the ladies.

He agreed to school this one, got it bending its neck and going on the bit, and then faced it at a small fence. At the very last moment it tried to run out. Frank, with much stronger leg aids than the owner would have had, managed to keep it in but in doing so his knee cartilage was torn. He was in horrendous pain, and the damage turned out to be so bad that Frank never rode again. His dreams of riding with his grandchildren at home in Ireland were dashed. Being unable to ride, he also gave up being a show jumping owner and trainer, although he continued judging right until 2005 at which time his eyesight was no longer good enough.

19

A Man of Many Parts

In December 1988 Frank McGarry announced to a surprised show jumping world in general, and the Connaught region in particular, that he was not going to put himself forward for re-election, for the first time in 35 years.

Michael Slavin in *The Irish Field* of 17 December 1988 explained:

> *It is not because he would not like to [stand]. It is not because he is no longer enthusiastic about his sport... His complaint begins where the Association has its roots – in the regions. As far as he is concerned, too much time is spent in regional meetings discussing matters that have already taken hours of discussion at national level.*

He felt the national executive should discuss national matters, and that the local regions should concentrate on local issues.

'Frank wants more time spent helping local shows and events and not to have every region trying to be the national executive, worrying about the whole country.'

Frank also considered there was too much canvassing for votes for the sake of power, rather than for the sake of the sport.

'Winning around the world with our horses is more important than winning an argument around a committee table,' he said.

Although Frank owned one or two racehorses in his time – and inevitably sold them on – he only occasionally went racing himself. For his colours (silks) he chose the red and white of Sligo Rovers.

Frank always supported his local Sligo Harriers point-to-point, and would sometimes enter a couple of his show jumpers to help fill up the numbers in the hunt members' race. One of the first was not a show jumper.

Frank was joint-Master of the Sligo Harriers

It came about when Frank was buying some cattle in Bal-lymahon, County Longford in about the late 1950s when he was offered a horse for sale. It was standing nearly up to its hocks in a big manure pit so the vendor, not aware that Frank knew about anything other than cattle, got the shock of his life when Frank, from some distance away, pointed out that it had a spavin.

Nevertheless, he bought it for £100 and sold it on to Andy Dodd for hunting. It was a thoroughbred called Paddy Brannagan, and he proved too hot for Andy so Frank took it back. The horse was a handful and ran away with Frank a couple of times. He was not suitable for show jumping so Frank ran him in a point-to-point which he won as he liked.

He was then put in training with Mick Kilfeather and looked like winning at Sligo until running so wide on the bends that he squandered first place. Nevertheless, Frank sold him to Willie Rooney, for whom he won numerous point-to-points. His daughter, Ann Ferris, won a point-to-point on him in Strabane when she was about 15 years old.

'He pulled my arms out,' she remembers, adding, 'Frank was always good fun and a good laugh.'

Frank bought a mare called Golden Curl from Harry Johnston, a draper, and she won a number of races for Billy Hunter and then for Frank. Another was a gelding called Killery. The North Mayo Harriers had asked him to give them a runner and Frank said, 'I don't have anything to gallop around but sure I'll take up that fella anyway and it'll be an entry. I thought it had no possible chance of winning.'

There were four runners. One fell at the first fence, one out in the country and the other had the race at its mercy when it, too, fell at the last fence, leaving Frank's horse only having to gallop through the finish to win.

He recalls the time a man of about 40, John Rogers from Ballymoate, came to the riding school to learn to ride. He was very keen and after 15 lessons he said he wanted to buy a horse. Frank advised that he should get something sensible that was good on roads, like a nice old cob. Instead, Rogers went to the thoroughbred sales. A colt came in, and the auctioneer was looking for £2,000 for it, then £1,000 then, still with no bid, he called out, as auctioneers do, 'won't anybody give me £100 for this Tiepolo gelding?'

Now it happened that the previous year Rogers had bought a piebald donkey stallion for £110 and had covered more than a hundred donkey mares with it at £10 a time. So now, on impulse, he put his hand up. No one else bid, and the colt was his for £100. In his ignorance, he hadn't realised the yearling had curbs (bony growths that can cause unsoundness) on both his hind hocks, and that was why no one had bid.

When he returned, Frank wouldn't even look at the youngster, and Rogers asked what he should do with it. Frank advised him to get it broken.

John Rogers recalls: 'About a few days later after the sales, the Duchess of Westminster happened to be in Paddy Kerins yard in Colloney, and while there she saw my yearling and said to Paddy that despite his curbs, he would win races. When I was told this later I found it hard to believe, but I started to believe it "could" happen someday. He was then sent to the Darroon Stud, owned by my great friend Paddy Healy, to be fed and brought to a fantastic two-year-old. Now because I had young children, I could not afford to keep him, so I asked my brother Michael if he would take a half share in him, and with a lot of persuasion he joined me.'

After he was broken in, the horse, now named Gay Tie, went into training with Donnie O'Keefe in Buttevant, County

Cork. He charged £20 per week at a time when top trainers' fees were considerably more.

At the end of the year Frank met John Rogers in a shop on Christmas Eve, and was told that Gay Tie was running at Limerick on the day after Stephen's Day, and to have a few quid on. He had run in a point-to-point as a three-year-old and had just been touched off by a horse ridden by Ted Walsh. Frank thought no more of it, but Gay Tie won the Adare novice chase as a four-year-old in Limerick.

John Rogers says, 'He was backed from 20-1 to 9-1 by trainer friends and our three cars full of family and friends. It was said to me that Donnie O Keeffe bought the OK Corral in Buttervant from his bet!'

After this race, Frank received a call from one of Ireland's leading trainers, Mick O'Toole, asking Frank to buy the horse for him.

'I thought it would be about £3,000 to £4,000 but they wanted £10,000. But Mick said he was worth buying, so he came down and bought him.'

Less than three months later, now owned by Dr P. Morrissey and trained by Mick O'Toole, he won the prestigious four-mile National Hunt Chase for amateur riders at the Cheltenham Festival, ridden by John Fowler.

John Rogers says, 'It just goes to show what you can do with a £110 race horse. O'Toole sold him for around £30,000, (nice profit in two months) but unfortunately he got injured a while later, and never ran again.'

Frank kept a few racehorses in training with a friend, Colonel Sean Daly, who kept a yard near the Phoenix Park where Ruby Walsh Sr., another friend of Daly's, trained at that time. He was also the chef d'equipe for the Army show jumping team for a number of years.

'Sean Daly was always trying to persuade me to buy a racehorse, and one day he told me he had one for me called Cold Scent. He wasn't big money and I wasn't really interested but I said I would have him.'

Some while later Frank was at Daly's stables where he noticed 'a horrible looking yoke in the third stable that was weaving and box walking, and nearly everything you could have wrong with a horse was wrong with him'. It was his horse.

'Well, I'll not be leading that one into the winner's enclosure,' Frank said. 'He's a terrible looking thing.'

Frank, usually tied up with show jumping, never once went to see him race – yet the horse won three or four times, including twice in one day on the strand in Laytown, County Meath, the only officially recognised beach races.

'So he wasn't a bad old horse at all, and I sold him to an English client.'

Frank next bought a mare by Vulgan called Kay's Vulgan and she won several races, yet he never saw her win. The time he was there to watch her she was beaten in a photo finish in Punchestown. Kay's Vulgan was then sold for roughly double what he had initially paid to Neil Wates (of the big Wates building company) and, ridden by Neil himself, she proved a star on the South East of England point-to-point scene for a number of years.

'I had said to Sean Daly that if you buy me a really good-looking horse I'll lead him in. He told me Sir Hugh Nugent had one to sell, a two-year-old colt called Sandyment. I paid good money for him, about £6,000, which was very big money, but I really liked him, and I said I'd like to back him when he was going to win.'

The horse campaigned initially in France and won a good race during the same week as the Prix de l'Arc de Triomphe in early October.

Frank didn't go, but unbeknown to him a fellow called Tim Corcoran, who happened to be the manager of the Southern Hotel in Sligo, was there, and had what he thought was a small bet on the horse, without realising that the value of the franc had changed, so when he put on what he thought was a tenner it was actually one hundred francs. The horse won at 16-1, and back in Sligo, Frank, not knowing Tim Corcoran, booked a table for dinner at the hotel. To his surprise, he found a bottle of champagne on the table.

Frank told the waitress it was not intended for him. She disappeared and returned to say it was for him. Tim Corcoran then came and introduced himself and explained what had happened.

Sandyment returned to Ireland but, with restrictions to racing due to the 1967 Foot and Mouth Disease, he was gelded and turned away. When he returned to training he ran down the field on his racing comeback; then he was laid out for a race at Clonmel. With his Irish form poor and his French win either not known about or ignored he started at 25-1. Once more Frank could not go, and neither could trainer Sean Daly because, in charge of Army transport, his duties required him to go down with vehicles to the Tuskar Rock plane crash tragedy of March 1968. Tim Corcoran went and Frank asked him to put on £5,000 for him.

In the race Sandyment looked like winning by the proverbial street when he broke down (strained a tendon) at the second last flight.

'He was a good horse,' Frank says, 'and we thought he would win a number of races. He was good looking and I would have liked to lead him in, but in the end I never led in any winner of mine.'

Frank rates Bula the greatest hurdler of all time, and he has special reason for remembering him.

'I went to Westport a number of times to help them start up a show. The meetings went on until 10.00 p.m. and I drove hundreds of miles in all, but they were a great committee, and anything that I suggested needed doing would be done. There was a man on the committee who had petrol station in Westport, Pongo Kelly, who wanted to learn to drive a horse. I got him a driving whip and he was like a child with a toy. He was a great man for having a few jars.'

One November Frank was surprised to bump into Pongo at the Goffs Sales that were then situated opposite the RDS in Dublin.

Jumping at Westport Show – vet Dermot Dolan from Longford has a bird's-eye view

'He was falling over with drink early in the morning. The first lot to come in was a two-year-old filly that was knocked down to him for £100.'

The filly was despatched by train for Westport, a journey that took four days because for three days the filly was lost in the wagon. When Pongo realised what he had bought he was aghast, and told Frank that at all costs he must hide the purchase from his wife. He asked Frank to help him get rid of it, and the upshot was that a Westport vet and amateur rider, Mark Scully, looked at the breeding, noted that she was a great-granddaughter of Triple Crown winner Gainsborough, and thought she would make a racehorse; he agreed to take her.

The filly's name was registered fittingly as Pongo's Fancy, and in time Mark Scully entered her for an amateur hurdle race at the Galway Festival. Mark rode her and won the race, after which it was discovered that Pongo's Fancy was in foal to a good sire called Raincheck. The brown colt that she foaled was to be named Bula.

As a three-year-old Bula was bought by Captain Bill Edwards-Heathcote in Dublin in 1968 for 1,350 guineas, and subsequently put into training with Fred Winter in the summer of 1969. He became one of the all-time NH greats, winning 34 of his 51 races, including the Champion Hurdles of 1971 and 1972, and progressing to a number of steeplechase wins. In 1977 he fell heavily in the two-mile Champion Chase at Cheltenham and two months later had to be put down.

Although racing did not play a big part in Frank's life he nevertheless was a founding shareholder in the current Sligo Racecourse that opened in 1955.

Hunting was a natural part of Frank's show jumping life offering a great education for a young horse, teaching it to pick its feet up, to jump out of awkward places, to learn about noise and excitement and buzz. It was also a useful market place for both buying and selling.

'In the early days we could take six show jumpers up to Banbridge for the opening show of the season and we could come home with five hunters. The opposition was always hot there and it sorted our potential jumpers out,' Frank says.

In the mid-1960s the Sligo Hounds hunt needed an infusion of fresh blood.

Gone were the days when Miss Constance Gore Booth, later Countess Markievicz, was described out hunting with the Sligo Harriers by Mr E. Rowlette of Cash in Sligo in the late 1870s as:

> ... a little girl her hair flowing about her shoulders, mounted on a small pony, I first saw her hunting with the County Sligo Harriers. I remember watching a good hunt in Ballincar when she rode right up with the huntsman, giving him perhaps somewhat less 'law' at his fences than the strict etiquette of the occasion prescribed. Never indeed allowing his horse more than a couple of lengths lead during any part of the run. I remember some of the fences they jumped. I have sometimes seen them jump since, but never without considerable self-congratulation by thsefew who got over safely. I have never known any woman whose skill in riding to hounds equals that of Ms Goore-Booth. I am doubtful whether I ever knew any man who was an all round better rider.

Frank recalls that Joe McMullen, 'a really nice man', wanted to see the Sligo Harriers back to former glory. In the shake-up that followed, Pat Britton (Frank's solicitor) became chairman, Brenda Anderson the secretary (she continued hunting until in her eighties and then unfortunately broke her back), Jan Prins from the Channel Islands joint-Master and huntsman, and Frank joint-Master. Jan agreed to look after the hounds, and Frank took care of seeing the farmers – he knew most of them through his cattle business – and the social side.

Frank and fellow joint-Master of the Sligo Harriers Jan Prins

The first thing to do was to get a pack of hounds together. At that point the remaining existing hounds needed to be put down, Frank says, rather than be allowed to roam loose around the countryside. He rang around and got together a few hounds from his friends Granville Nugent, Master of the North Down Harriers, and Billy McCully, Master of the East Down Foxhounds, and by November 1, the traditional opening of the hunting season, a new pack had been put together.

It was 1966, and at first there were half a dozen followers but by the season's end they were looking for further country to hunt across. Frank and his colleagues spent many months obtaining permission from farmers for access. After three years the hunt had become so popular with 100 people wanting to take part that a ticket system was introduced, whereby riders had to elect on which days they were going to hunt.

Frank was joint-master with Jan Prins for 17 seasons. It was through hunting that he got to know John Huston. Other regulars in the hunting field were John Brooke, son of Northern Ireland's premier, and his wife, Rosemary, who used to come to his house for drinks and a shower at the end of the day.

There was an occasion out hunting when Frank jumped into a thatched shed, an incident recalled by another guest that day, Diana Conolly-Carew.

'He jumped a stone wall without realising a thatched shed lay below it on the other side. The horse landed with his front legs firmly embedded in the thatch; it took a long time to get it out and it was such a fright.'

Frank recalls a time when a follower asked a farmer if he knew if the gentry had gone by.

'Yes,' the farmer replied, quick as a flash, 'about 150 years ago.'

Often the horses would be prepared and driven to the meet by Cecil Mahon and Francie Kerins, who both also hunted, and Frank would drive direct to the meet after feeding about 300 cattle in the sheds. Before long three of his children were also hunting, and Niall became keenest, continuing to hunt for many years.

'There's nothing like the country air, the whole Irish scene, what a place to bring up children, there are ponies to ride, there's nothing else on their mind, a bit of a hunt across the country, doing no damage to anybody.'

He adds, 'The great thing about the hunting fraternity is there's no prize at the end, unlike show jumping, but hunting is totally and utterly a sport and everybody is out for a day's fun and you'd meet some of the loveliest people.'

One of the characters he remembers was Howard Temple of McGee's of Donegal, 'a lovely old character', and another was a vet called Andrew Dodd, who hunted in Sligo for 57 years and

Frank hunting on St Stephen's Day from
Redgate Crossroads, early 1960s

was 'a wonderful, colourful character'. It was Andrew Dodd's yard in Sligo that Frank had rented for many years before he bought Carrowmore. He always 'took a few drinks', and one of the traditions that quickly became established was a get together at the end of the day.

'I'd come home in the evening and have a good hot bath and a glass of brandy then a bunch of us would go out to dinner in the Great Southern Hotel or the Moorings Restaurant.'

Over the evening the day's fences, of course, got bigger and bigger, and the falls more dramatic.

When Frank retired from the Mastership in 1980, having held that post since 1966, a dinner-dance was held for 200 people, and Frank was presented with a Waterford glass vase. He was followed by Kieran Horohan, Muriel Siberry and Derek Pugh. In time he was pleased to see some of the children he had taught at the riding school taking their part in the hunt.

Frank says simply, 'My hunting days were probably the best days of my life.'

There was very little in equestrianism that Frank did not achieve, and this included in the showing world.

Possibly the best show horse he ever produced was Irish King, who won 29 classes and was overall champion 29 times, with the added bonus that he was home-bred, out of a mare called Bang On. When the horse was a youngster, Frank told Diana Conolly-Carew, who was on the team with him in Madrid, that he had a horse at home who would win the championship in Dublin. Although a show jumper, Diana was also a highly accomplished show rider and she relished that particular thought. On their return she and her mother, Lady Carew, came to see him.

When they arrived they were astonished, believing the horse looked unlikely to win any championship let alone the premier accolade. But they took up Frank's offer to show the newly broken four-year-old for him, and with no alternative available Frank entered him in the opening show of the season at Balmoral.

He promptly won not only his class but also the overall championship. Frank missed it as he was on another part of the ground with the show jumpers. He was approached by a journalist and asked how it felt to win the supreme championship.

Frank replied, 'I feel the biggest eejit in Balmoral, because I didn't enter him for the ladies, and all he'd have to do was walk in to win it.'

Next morning Frank read in the *Belfast Telegraph* words to the effect that Frank McGarry says he feels the biggest eejit in Balmoral.

Frank also rode Irish King himself at a number of shows until eventually he sold him to Tommy Brennan, and from there he moved on to Germany where Frank believes he reached the Olympics in dressage.

'He was poetry in motion,' Frank says.

Diana Conolly-Carew's older brother, Patrick, also won a prestigious showing class for Frank at the Champions of the Year on Irish Rover in 1966.

Diana Conolly-Carew's chief international show jumper was the grey, Barrymore, but she also competed abroad on a further ten jumpers. She was the first woman to be part of Ireland's winning Nations Cup team for the Aga Khan cup in 1963. She rode in the 1968 Mexico Olympics with Barrymore.

Errigal, who was bought from Frank, was her main speed horse, but she then lent him to Paul Darragh for the junior team, and in the Junior European Championships they won an Individual silver medal in Dinard in 1969 and Individual bronze the next year in St Moritz (he won another silver in Hickstead in 1971 on Woodpecker 11). Paul, as we have seen, went on to be in four winning Aga Khan Cup teams from 1976-79, but died in 2005 at only 51 years old, a great loss to Irish show jumping.

Diana, in addition to her show jumping, holds the distinction of having won showing championships at the RDS for show pony, hack, small hunter, working hunter and supreme hunter, a remarkable feat.

In 1985 Diana married Baron Alexis Wrangle, son of the last White Russian general who with the European Allies helped save hundreds of thousands of civilians, soldiers and priests from the ravages of the Red Army. Baron Wrangle died in 2005.

Although Diana's older brother, Lord Carew, is better known as a three-day event rider, he was one of those rare horsemen who, like Tommy Brennan, was also an international show jumper. He rode in both the Mexico and Munich Olympic Games event team of 1968 and 1972, and was chef d'equipe in Montreal in 1976; he rode in Badminton horse trials ten times and was a member of the FEI Bureau for eight years; he was an eventing judge for more than twenty years; and was president of the Grand Jury (senior judge) for eventing at the Olympic Games of 1992 and 1996.

20

A Surprise Offer

Frank was very young when he became a show judge. It is sometimes said that it is only possible to please one person in a showing class, and that is the winner; it is not a case of first past the post or an exact science but of a judge's own preference.

There was a time when Frank put up a weedy, light young thoroughbred that was small but well put together ahead of a well matured and rounded Irish draft yearling at Ballinamore Show. The owner of the runner-up sought out Frank afterwards and quite a heated discussion ensued. Frank said he would like to know how both had turned out in three years.

'The little one is all quality and some day will turn out good.'

It happened that in time he found out. The runner-up had made the good price of £700. The little light one, however, named Leitrim, was sold to the Army for £6,000 and won the Imperial Cup in White City, London, with Colonel Campion riding.

Although Frank judged hunters at a number of shows it was as a show jumping judge that he did most. He could sometimes judge at as many as 73 shows in a year. One colleague, Ado

Kenny, says he spent many enjoyable hours in judges' boxes for some forty years with Frank.

'The first time I ever judged a competition was with Frank; I learned more from watching him and listening than I would have done from any book. He was a believer in common sense and giving the competitor the benefit of any doubt. If some new young competitors needed to be spoken to regarding dress or behaviour it was never done publicly but quietly and kindly outside the ring.'

Ado continues, 'He entertained his fellow judges in the box with a constant flow of good natured banter and an endless repertoire of yarns, but he never missed anything that went on in the arena.'

There was a time in later years when Ado was running a few shows and he became embroiled in a wrangle with the SJAI over a car prize for a rider.

'Frank was one of the few who supported me at executive meetings, and I never could understand why so many opposed the car prize. Eventually that matter was resolved and I was delighted to see Frank award a car prize at his equitation centre in Sligo.'

Ado judged there himself many times and says, 'It was a top of the range place – a great viewing balcony with a glass partition overlooking the arena and a bar for spectators, owners and riders, probably the first to have such facilities.'

He adds, 'Frank was a great judge of a horse, and of cattle. The late Jimmy Connon often told me how good he was at picking out the best cattle at a fair.'

Frank began judging in Dublin in about 1968, along with people such as Louis McGee, Frank O'Reilly and Granville Nugent, as well as John Wiley, Paddy Dunne Cullenan and Eddie Boylan.

Frank judging in Omagh with Hugh McCusker

Frank also did a lot of the announcing at shows all around the country, and in Dublin until announcing became a specific job.

He recalls a time he needed a new crash bowler hat and on the Monday after Dublin Show he took himself off to Kingstons in O'Connell Street. There, an assistant asked him his head size, and Frank told him six and three-quarters, which is small. The assistant popped into the back of the shop several times and each time returned to ask Frank his head size again. Eventually, the assistant called the manager. Once more, Frank was asked for his head size and Frank told him, adding, 'I have had this head since I was born.'

The manager replied, 'Be Jaysus, it's only a pimple, it never came to a head.'

Breeding was a sideline to Frank – we have seen that his 13.2 hand high Irish Peach produced top class competition horses – but he was hot on its importance to the Irish horse abroad. There was a time in the mid-1960s when the pool gene of Irish Draft mares had almost disappeared because so many had been sold abroad. This was a matter he tried to address when he was on the Irish Horse Board.

'I was always interested in trying to produce, or seeing that Ireland produced, a three-quarter to seven-eighths part blood horse from the foundation stock of Irish Draft crossed with a thoroughbred to try and get jumpers.'

He felt the right stallions were the key. A bad mare could produce one bad foal a year, but a bad stallion could sire a hundred – and he 'wasn't on for bringing in any foreign-breds'.

His idea was that the board should buy the top five yearling colts at most shows in the country and bring them along in an umbrella centre. He discussed his dream with Charlie Haughey, who was then Minister for Agriculture. He wanted the umbrella organisation to have under it the various societies for Connemara ponies, Kerry ponies, Irish Draft horses and so on – anything except racing which was a separate entity. He wanted an establishment with sufficient stabling and means to produce the top youngsters, performance test them at two or three years old, and send those with most potential out to various trainers.

He feels now that the very markets they would have been aiming for, America and Japan, are instead buying warm-bloods from Holland, France and Germany.

When he was marketing manager on the board the English, Italians, Swedish and Swiss already bought a lot of Irish horses. Frank was also determined to sell to the oil countries of the Middle East.

'We advertised in Kuwait, Syria and Libya, and we did sell a lot of horses out to Saudi and the Emirates, they were very good customers.'

The board was disbanded in 1981 before he could achieve his dreams, but he is pleased to see the way things are going now, with performance stallions in Ireland.

Cruising was an example of a good performing show jumper who sired many top horses.

Frank says, 'The amazing thing is his sire, Seacrest, wasn't passed by the board and his dam, Mullacrew [by the thoroughbred Nordlys], was given to the board by the Army. She was a very good show jumper and jumped internationally. Eventually we [the board] agreed to give her to Mary McCann for breeding.'

Cruising died in September 2014. He won many Grand Prix classes ridden by Trevor Coyle, as well as being on a number of winning Nations Cups teams in the 1990s.

What was really needed in order to produce athletic horses that would go to the top, Frank believed, was a subsidy from the Government for the right stallions. There was too much breeding by chance, he felt, adding that the small farmer couldn't afford an expensive stallion, hence the need for backing.

In the mid-1990s, a few years into his show jumping retirement, Frank received a tempting offer to revamp and run the sport in Dubai.

'What the sheiks really wanted was for me to re-organise their show jumping, especially their rules and regulations in the whole of the Emirates.'

He was offered £250,000 a year, plus car and driver. In addition he was told they would build him a house and provide a housekeeper. They wanted him to come immediately for two months.

Frank told them he couldn't just drop everything, but a week later they provided a plane ticket from Dublin to Amsterdam to Abu Dhabi. When he arrived at Amsterdam he didn't have a visa for the onward journey.

'A big screen was put around me, and I was told I couldn't go into the country. I said I had an invitation from the Sheik.'

The next thing Frank knew was there were about six people around him saying, 'this is your bleep, your phone, your driver, your interpreter, your hotel.' He spent the next two months at the Sheraton Hotel in Abu Dhabi.

It all seemed very tempting, but as far as Frank was concerned there was a problem. He says, 'I didn't understand them. They wouldn't turn up for meetings and they didn't seem to care; they had too much money.'

When he did manage to get to meetings he found them disorganised and higgledy piggledy.

'They all had great big bricks of mobile phones and smoked all through dinner. They offered to build me a house wherever I liked and to furnish it. I was tempted because in two years I would have made a lot of money. Then they said they wanted me to buy horses in France, and I said no, you can't do that, and I turned down the job. I wanted to go home to my land and horses and family, but they tried to tempt me. Eventually they came to Ireland to buy, but not from me.'

Frank recommended them the perfect person instead in Lt Col Ronnie McMahon, and he went in 1999, with someone else in between.

Ronnie McMahon had joined the Irish Army at 18 specifically to be involved in its famed School of Equitation at the McKee Barracks in the Phoenix Park. He had been a winner with Irish junior teams and his first major Dublin call-up was as part of an Army team competing against both a civilian side and a British side in a competition arranged domestically due to a ban on horse travel to the continent in 1966, as Swamp Fever had broken out.

He toured Europe and North America with the Army team, and in 1971, with Ned Campion and Billy Ringrose, he won the Nations Cup in Fontainbleau, France. He persuaded the Army to diversify into eventing and represented Ireland in the Olympic Games in Munich in 1972 and Montreal in 1976.

In 1999, having served as trainer and two years as Officer in Command at McKee Barracks, Lt Col McMahon officially retired, and it was then that he went to Dubai as adviser and head of the UAE Equestrian and Racing Federation.

21

Frank's Legacy

Frank's love of good horses and cattle has sustained him throughout his life, as have the fine horsemen and women he has met along the way.

His mottos have been, 'I never wanted to get fat' (which with his zest for work he never did). 'The most important thing to me, buying or selling, was hold on to your good name,' a total honesty in dealing – and there is no one who would deny he was true to that. Finally, he says, 'Always to be the best.'

Many newspaper articles have heaped praise upon him, his horses, and the work he has done for Irish show jumping.

- Sligo Man Put West of Ireland on Show Jumping Map – contributed towards Ireland's International reputation for horses, 1963, *Sligo Champion*

- Irish jumping team made big impression abroad, 1964, *Irish Independent*

- Sligo horses earn worldwide fame (1980s)

- The Master Returns – Frank Makes His Mark in America, 1989, *Sligo Champion*

- McGarry – a man of many stories, *Irish Field*, Michael Slavin, 1988

- Connacht honours Frank McGarry, the Irish Horse (*Farmers Journal*), Frank Mulvihill, 2004

- The leading man in Irish show jumping, *Connaught Tribune*, Stephen Glen, about 2007

With the exception of Go-Sly-Up, 'the horse who couldn't stop winning,' who was a cob, albeit a very good stamp, Frank would almost invariably go for good looking and well-bred animals.

'I wouldn't usually have much time for a plain horse. I like quality and would buy as near to thoroughbred as possible or three-quarter bred.'

The competitive spirit also never left Frank. He recalls a time when he was being interviewed by a reporter in Spain, and he was asked, 'Do you really go out to win a competition?'

Francie Kerins and Frank receiving a Waterford Crystal trophy from a Guinness representative at Longford Show

Frank replied, 'I'm not interested in second, third or fourth place, all right though they might be. My intention is to win, although as a good sport I also hate to see the other fella lose.'

More than anything he still gets a thrill from watching a fine horse win a top competition, or a race or point-to-point, and equally he hates to see a good horse beaten, such as Arkle or Bula. He rates Sprinter Sacre possibly the best racehorse he has ever seen. 'I cried when he won the 2012 Queen Mother Champion Chase. I was sitting here alone at home watching it on television. There's nothing like it when you see a perfect model do what he's meant to do.' And he includes Dundrum along with a Canadian horse called Hickstead among the best show jumpers.

'But it does happen that they get beaten and you have to put up with it. When you have the likes of little Red Rum who won the Grand National three times, or Boomerang who was a fantastic show jumper for Eddie Macken, they are the types you don't like to see beaten, but it does happen.'

He goes on to muse about his lifelong involvement in horses.

'I suppose I took a hand at nearly every section of equestrianism from six years old when I began riding donkeys, and progressed to small ponies in traps and carts. I carted with ponies to the bog and usually rode them home and very often would slip out in the evening after a full day carting and ride around the fields and pop over a couple of walls.'

He also did some local eventing and hunter trials, as well as show riding and hunting.

Although Frank never rode internationally, because in the early days he was too busy creating his cattle business and thereafter in the administration of the sport, he nevertheless always enjoyed riding at home, as we have seen with his involvement with the Sligo Harriers (in which almost inevitably he also took an executive role), and in the show ring.

Amongst the people he has known in his chosen sport, he singles out Tommy Wade, Tommy Brennan and Leslie Fiztpatrick 'all fantastic horsemen,' Colonel Billy Ringrose, Ned Campion, Seamus Hayes, Con Power, Larry Kiely, 'he was a lovely fella, they were all lovely fellas to travel with, and later Gerry Mullins [who was part of the winning Aga Khan Cup team in 1981], and John Leddy [Ledingham], they all got wonderful results for Ireland.'

Frank says that today Ireland boasts about 22 of the world's top show jumpers, including 19-year-old Bertram Allen. 'He's a smashing young rider.'

Leslie Fitzpatrick was a wholesale jeweller in Grafton Street, Dublin with his father. He grew up with ponies, starting with Iris Kellett, and had a very good pony called Mac D. He graduated to horses and was good enough to go on that first civilian team to Ostend and Rotterdam.

Leslie Fitzpatrick says, 'When Frank built the new riding school it was on top of the world. We always partied well in addition to it being a good show; Frank was great fun and very knowledgeable, with a great family.'

Frank says, 'I often stayed with Leslie in Stillorgan. Francie and Cecil would take my horses up on a Saturday, and Leslie's grooms would have stables bedded down ready. He was a brilliant host, and 100 per cent efficient; he was always very generous to me over the years. I have much to thank him for.'

Frank wrote a poem for Leslie on the occasion of his marriage, and his father, B-J, gave Frank a Waterford crystal chandelier when he built his house at Carrowmore.

Tommy Brennan died in July 2014, aged 74 years. He was a rare sportsman in that he rode for his country in two different disciplines: he achieved an individual fourth place for show jumping in the 1964 Tokyo Olympics with Kilkenny, and two years later they went on to achieve a team eventing gold medal in the 1966 World Championship Three Day Event at Burghley, a feat that Tommy considered the highlight of his career.

In 1997 he was inducted into the Irish Sports Council Hall of Fame for Services to Equestrian Sport, following the Gold Badge of Honour he received from the world governing body, the FEI, in 1985.

Winner of nine RDS National Championships and some 64 international competitions, Tommy drew international

Tommy Brennan and Frank – officials wear top hat and tails for the Aga Khan trophy at the RDS Dublin Horse Show

praise for his design of the European Eventing Championships course at Punchestown in 1991. He went on to design
the Punchestown course again in 2003, and he became much
sought after throughout Ireland for designing imaginative
hunter trial courses.

Frank knew Tommy from a teenager, and apart from being
a fine horseman and outgoing character, he also won the title
of Young Farmer of the Year.

Tommy was great fun on the tours and he and Frank remained in regular contact with weekly phone calls right until
the time of his death. Frank chatted with him the night before
he died when Tommy told him he was coming home the next
day.

'He was probably the best and easiest guy you could have
on a team, and he would listen to you, if we were discussing the
number of strides between fences, for instance. He was flam-
boyant and he loved a jar – and he was a good horseman.'

A few years ago Frank wrote a poem about Tommy Brennan.

Of a friend and colleague I must write,
A man of grit and fame
I class this man among the best.
Tom Brennan is his name.
His heart was given to a sport, a horse was by his side,
Show jumping was the name of it, where Tommy loved to ride.

He travelled to the Continent in those early days,
And helped to win the Nations Cups
With Leslie, Wade and Hayes.
When speed it was a factor he was always at his best
And he left for dead all famous names
The trophy to arrest.

If he lost by half a second the chef d'equipe got blame,
Whose views were sometimes different, but
Our interests were the same.

We then might start discussing the girls
And how to sin,
But we finished talking horses and planning how to win.

I've been asked on most occasions, his ability in the ring,
My answer it was loud and prompt
Of course he was the king.
D'Inzeo and Pessoa and Schockemöhle, too
When asked that very question
Say we all agree with you.

My best experience of this man
Was a show in Amsterdam,
A car for first on offer, to win it
Was the plan.
The horse's name was Donegal to beat the world's best
Which Tommy did in unique style with splendour and with zest.

A legend in eventing, to the pinnacle
He did go
And captured world markings at the
Games in Mexico.
When celebrations started Tom was always there
To represent his country in that beverage affair.

The life achievements that were his
Which money couldn't buy,
His talent to it was unique, how we
All love this guy.
We still sit around in rings at night discussing all his fame
And all Ireland laud his accolades and sing Tom Brennan's
  name.

Of horses that he produced, especially his 22 International horses, he has many special memories. He singles out Errigal, Westcourt, Sensation, Pleasant Knight, Oatfield Hills and two ridden by his son, Declan, Nephin Mor and the pony Curraghill. And of course the one horse he never sold, Go-Sly-Up.

'They were all fantastic horses.'

Ask him what was his most special win and he replies all of them, but then he picks out one particular day, the 1966 Malahide Champions of the Year Show, an indoor competition for the title show jumper of the year. He took three horses, and won with all three: the puissance with a small mare called GiGi (dam of Sligo GiGi), ridden by Francie Kerins, and the Grand Prix-type championship class with Oatfield Hills. In the show ring Pat Carew won the Champion Show Horse of the Year on Frank's Irish Rover. Frank has a solid silver tray given by Watneys Beers to remember the occasion by.

Frank is someone who from boyhood always knew his own mind and set about achieving his aims, and managed this without crossing swords on a personal level. He is a fine example of a man who is true to himself and dedicated to his chosen path. He is held not only in high regard but also with endearment in the Irish equestrian world.

As the late Tommy Brennan said, 'He was an ordinary man who did extraordinary things.'

Frank's tireless work for the sport of show jumping, equestrianism generally and cattle was always honorary. He never claimed expenses for the thousands of miles he drove to meetings or to shows where he was judging.

'I was pleased to make a contribution to the shows; it was the same with the SJAI where my intention was to help set it up and bring in the rules.'

He says, 'I loved all of it and gave most of my time to it. I remember at one particular stage, beginning to wonder what I was giving my life to. Was it totally to meetings and rules and regulations and judging?'

GiGi in Dublin

He was on the executive of the Show Jumping Association of Irish and was chairman of the Connaught region. The SJAI chairmanship rotated between the four regions but he never took it up because, with so many other commitments, he did not feel he could give it the necessary time.

He was a selector for the international Irish show jumping team for some seventeen years. One of the most successful innovations during his terms of office was the introduction of the Farrier Scheme. At the time farriers were in short supply and the Board placed apprentices with existing farriers for three years, paid for by the Scheme.

He was chairman of the executive committee of the Cattle Traders Association and of the Cattle Association of Sligo, and of the Western Livestock Exporters Company.

'I never charged anybody anything in my lifetime, but some shows would send me a present, and I might get a piece of Waterford glass or something like that, which was lovely.'

Plenty of accolades deservedly came Frank's way during his life, including various civic receptions and parades. He was Sligo Man of the Year 1974 and received into the Hall of Fame in 1979. In 1984 he was officiating, as usual, at Ballina Show in County Mayo when he was told there was a phone call for him. He walked from the judges' box to the far end of the showground only to find there a coach and four waiting to take him and Francie Kerins round the main ring in a lap of honour. The organisers had planned the surprise as an appreciation of their 35 years' support of the show, and he and Francie were both given a commemorative silver tray.

Frank was an International judge from 1964 until 2005, and an owner of show jumpers for 37 years. He was Ireland's leading owner 14 times, 13 consecutively from 1959, succeeding Jean Morrison from Derry, until 1972. He missed it in

Francie Kerins and Frank receiving a special award in Ballina, 1984 after being paraded round the ring in a coach and four – they are flanked by, on the left, Tiernan Gill, a member of the show committee, Peter Murphy and Peter Hanley

Frank in his trophy room

1973, but won again the next year. He notched an astonishing 5,000-plus wins as an owner in affiliated events. In 2004 he was recognised with a special presentation at the RDS Dublin Horse Show for 50 years of service.

His last contribution to show jumping administration was the ticket system which has been a great success for the SJAI and the competitor alike. It was a simple, fool-proof system that nevertheless took 16 years for it to be taken up after Frank first suggested it. In it every registered show jumper, complete with its ID/Passport is given a number for life or grade, even if it changes hands. The number is bar-coded so that any winnings go on to a computer and straight to head office.

'It means gone are the days of checking numbers in the collecting ring or peering to see the number on a rider's back,' says Frank.

When he was first judging, a rider might come into the ring of an affiliated class without the horse being registered; the judge was held responsible for allowing it to jump.

Frank insisted he was there as a judge, and that the stewards in the pocket should verify that the horses were registered. He came up with the 'cheque book' system that would give the horse's breeding, age, height, colour with a unique number for life. He took his suggestion to the chairman, Dr Alec Lyons.

At first, the SJAI said the scheme would cost too much; Frank countered that a bank cheque cost twopence. The idea was shelved until eventually, more than a dozen years later, it was decided that too many horses were jumping out of their class and officials weren't able to detect them. Only then was Frank's idea adapted and adopted into the ticketing system. Not only did it help the smooth running of a show, but it also ensured accurate results were given to the Press, and correct points and prize-money recorded for every horse.

'It's also much easier for the announcer as everything is there in print, he doesn't have to decipher illegible handwriting, so it's very simple and you can't make mistakes. It's barcoded, it can go into the computer and have results immediately. So I'm very proud that I did that. Lord Lowry once said I was twenty years ahead of my time.'

The same had been said by Charles Haughey in his speech when he opened the riding school. Since then, indoor arenas have proliferated nationwide.

*Paddy Shortt, Eithne McAughey, Frank
and Sean McAughey in Gran Canaria*

Lord Lowry was the highly regarded Lord Chief Justice of Northern Ireland. As the North's most senior judge he was three times the target of failed assassination attempts. An all-round sportsman known mainly for cricket and golf, his interest in show jumping came fairly late in life, when his skills led him to be a judge both in Ireland and abroad right up until shortly before his death. He was also chairman of the Judicial Committee of the International Equestrian Federation, and a member of the Jury of Appeal at the Olympic Games in Atlanta in 1996.

Part of Frank's lifelong enjoyment of show jumping was the sing-song that invariably took place after every international or major show. The Dublin Horse Show every August remains the annual highlight – there are many who consider it the best show in the world – not only for watching the cream of international show jumping and Irish-produced hunters but also for the wealth of old friends that he meets.

For a number of years, until he was 85, Frank drove a '91 Sligo maroon top-of-the-range Mercedes saloon, a type he has driven since 1959. Today, it is parked outside his apartment in Salthill, Galway, and is started periodically. Living in an apartment below him is Sean Donegan who has become a close friend.

Sean says, 'Frank is a man who has been friends with both kings and princes and never lost the common touch. He is a conversationalist of the first order; no-one can tell a story like him, his wit and joviality are legendary. He is a man of the highest integrity and honesty, and he is a kind and generous neighbour.'

Frank loves Sligo with a passion and he thrived in his involvement with show jumping, the people he met and inevitably, still the occasional cattle trade; dealing was as deep rooted in him as sleeping and thinking, but interestingly he says he was never a horse dealer. Show jumping was his hobby, cattle deal-

Gerry McGarry with Frank on his sister Josie's
90th birthday in 2009

ing his business. He says occasionally he sold horses either to help pay for the others (he kept a separate show jumping account), or if one simply wasn't good enough, or because he was given an offer he couldn't refuse.

'I always bought with the intention of improving a horse. If I thought one could make Grade A or International I would keep it; some lost money.'

In addition to his show jumping and cattle association posts he was also a member of the local drama society, and of course the riding school was special to him.

His domestic circumstances changed and in the mid-1990s Frank retired to a luxury apartment in Salthill, above Galway Bay, built by his nephew Gerry McGarry, where much of the floor in front of the sitting room hearth is taken up with a tapestry rug of Go-Sly-Up, the horse who couldn't stop winning. A few of his treasured trophies are on display (his home at Carrowmore had a whole room filled with trophies and he still ran out of space for them all.) Photographs abound on the windowsills and shelves and in albums.

Now, at 87, Frank McGarry has failing eyesight, but nothing dims that twinkle in his eye. He has family nearby and he often visits Carrowmore; he also still goes horse and cattle buying, usually with his nephew, Gerry. The dark months of winter are spent in the warmth of Gran Canaria in the company of long-time friends and family.

Nothing in his life can take that away.

Appendix 1

Frank McGarry's International Horses

Errigal

Go-Sly-Up

Westcourt

Sensation

Morning Melody

Irish Coast

Little Toi

Smokey Joe

Barnscourt

Oatfield Hills

Sligo Special

Nephen Mor

Sligo Supreme

Sligo Joker

Sligo Bells

On Rush On

Appendix 2

Frank McGarry's Riders

Seamus Gilmartin, first jumping pony

Hilda Togher, style and appearance classes

Monica Cleave

John Rowe

Declan McGarry

Donal Kerins

Francis Kerins

Mary-Rose Robinson

Tommy Brennan

Billy McCully

Kevin Moloney

Richard McDermott

Sean Ollef

Eddie Macken

Diana Connolly-Carew (Lady Wrangle) showing

Lord [Patrick] Carew showing

Lady [Anne] Hemphill showing

Jim McCawley

Cecil Mahon

Robert Burns

Maxie Scully

John Brake

Brian McNicholl

Barbara Bourne

Robert Splaine

Jenny Newall

Gerard O'Grady

With apologies from Frank for any he may have inadvertently omitted.

Appendix 3

A Selection of Frank McGarry's Poems

Thank You for the Morning

Thank you for the morning when I open first my eyes,
And also for my hearing of nature's moans and sighs.
The fragrance of the countryside comes with gift of smell,
My taste buds acting normal, thank God my all is well.

And then the daily work and chores, some good and evil too,
I just say thanks at midday, for all belongs to you.
And then the twilight comes along, the body seems to ache,
To compensate a query mind; I hope it's for God's sake.

I thank you for the limbs I use that take me through the day,
The heart through which the blood of life flows until you say,
The brawn and brains to progress, the hands to do their skill,
You gave me life and soul and hope, now let me do your will.

I thank you for the gift of speech and voice to tell Your song,
I hope t'will never slander give or quote against You wrong.
The will for to compose these lines, I know, belongs to You
And when I'm on the edge, my Lord, retrieve me and renew.

Our stay on earth is very short, declining with each day,
So realise the time is now, respite for just to say –
Thank you God for all I've got and what you have in store,
For my final days, be long or short, until I am no more.

This Life

Life is like a lucky bag with its many trades inside
It's up to you the one to choose
That you'll carry through with pride.
But the winds of change sometimes dictate
The way one's life should go
And your harvest will depend upon
Which type of seed you sow.

Some may choose a life of prayer,
And more the desk and pen.
Others face a life of crime, with drugs and drink and sin,
Some may like to farm the land
Produce our many crops,
More may join the boys in blue
As our regiment of cops.

Some will train as lawyers to represent us in the courts
More will train as athletes to play our many sports
And then the one we all dismissed
Who sailed right to the top
And became a model for us all, the vintage of the crop.

Then you get that wake-up call
You're not ready to relate,
You cannot leave this world behind,
And the wealth you did create.
So then you check the jigsaw,
Some parts all ain't there,
But time won't wait to find them
In a world you don't think fair.

Then one day the Master calls,
And He'll summon you to go,
Reluctantly you leave behind
All we've gathered here below.
But stop you must and realise
There's a message in that call,
That we only have the lend of these earthly goods.
That's all.

Ireland Tomorrow

I'm hoping to start a new party in the Dail
And my mind is puzzled to give it a name
Oh, God, it could not be called Fianna Fail,
Fine Gael, nor Labour, Sinn Fein.

Every person elected will be working for free
And the transport will be that of the State
I think I might call it the new Inisfree
And all the old boys get the gate.

We'll have a Minister for Anger, the first seat on our file
And Transport will be the next post
To take all the young people away from our soil,
Those who caused it in Hell they must roast.

We'll have a Minister for NAMA to get back our dough
And one post we must call it Hell
We'll get all the bankers and lawyers we know
And by God we'll give them a long spell.

We'll have a Minister for widows and old people, too
And we'll double their pensions as well;
Consultants, physicians cut their fees in two
And their perks we'll look into as well.

We'll have a Minister for condoms, single mothers look out
As your fun will sure be curtailed.
Single dads you must stop all this gaddin' about
As the dole office doors will be nailed.

The new jail will be ten times the size of Mountjoy,
Developers and builders will have to do time,
Thousands of wardens we'll have to employ
To make these boys repent of their crime.

Ministers Harney and Coughlan, Liz McManus if there,
Nora Owen and Joan Burton we'll bring along too
And we'll find that big hole in the ozone layer
And we'll stuff them in there till they stew.

We'll have a Minister for the Gardai to get them back to work
Big bellies and bums we'll decrease
Get them out on the street and the pubs they will shirk
More respect for the State should increase.

We'll have one for each county not called a TD,
Their work will be twelve hours a day,
If I just hear a mention of overtime fee
I'll bring a shipload of Indians each day.

Aer Lingus staff we'll give to RyanAir
And to Michael O'Leary we'll hand up the skies,
The new Terminal 2 will be free, I declare,
And landing fees we then can revise.

Outside the Dail we'll have a cremational big pit,
Michael D will burn well when he's high,
But wait till the Taoiseach is thrown on the spit
Sure the grease smoke will cloud the whole sky.

Denis O'Brien will come back to give us a hand-out
Ten billion in cash he'll declare,
In case of his licence we'd have any doubt
He'll refer us to Lowry or Desmond I'll swear.

We'll disband the unions, of that I am sure,
Then the workers are set to go free,
Have a mind of their own what job they'll procure
No dictation or big union fee.

I hope you'll all vote and give my party a start,
To get you out of that hole is my plea;
Put politicians and bankers in a space ship to Mars
Lock them in and throw me down the key.

Acknowledgements

Thanks go first and foremost to Frank McGarry for his patience, help and willingness in this project, which has been in his mind for a couple of decades; also to members of his family, including sons Niall and Declan and especially to his nephew Gerry; and to all those who have chatted to me about their friend for whom they have the greatest admiration, including Cecil Mahon, Francie Kerins, Brian McNicholl, Billy McCulley, Anthony McGarry, Leslie Fitzpatrick, Baroness Diana Wrangle (née Conolly-Carew), Lord Patrick Carew, Ann Ferris, Mervyn Clarke, Billy Ringrose, John Rogers, Noel C. Duggan, Ann Gormley, Jim Cawley, Lady Perdita Blackwood and Monica Flanagan.

My thanks also to members of the McGarry family for the use of photographs, and to Myles Quinn of Ballinagore Equestrian Centre for the author pic.

Frank's neighbour Sean Donegan deserves special mention as a reader to Frank and more besides.

A big thank you also to Ray MacSharry for writing the Foreword.

My appreciation goes also to David Givens of The Liffey Press for his belief in the story and the publishing of this book.

Ireland's Mr Show Jumping

Sources:

Carrowmore Megalithic Cemetery (Office of Public Works)

The Children of Castletown House, Sarah Conolly-Carew (The History Press Ireland) 2012

Connaught Tribune

http://www.constancemarkievicz.ie/

www.dublinhorseshow.com

The Farmers Journal

Horse and Hound

www.horsesportireland.ie

http://horsetalk.co.nz/archives

The Irish Field

The Irish Independent

Meath Chronicle

www.military.ie

http://www.newulsterbiography.co.uk/

http://www.rds.ie/

Show Jumping, Records, Facts and Champions, Judith Draper (Guinness Superlatives) 1987

Sligo Champion

http://www.sports-reference.com/

The World's Show Jumpers, Pamela Macgregor-Morris (Macdonald) 1955

Index